LIFE IS A PRISM

My Journey To Becoming Banker

AJAY SHASHIKANT MAHAJAN

BlueRose ONE.com
Stories Matter
NewDelhi • London

BLUEROSE PUBLISHERS
India | U.K.

BlueRose ONE
Stories Matter
NewDelhi • London

For permissions requests or inquiries regarding this publication, please contact:

BLUEROSE PUBLISHERS
www.BlueRoseONE.com
info@bluerosepublishers.com
+91 8882 898 898
+4407342408967

ISBN: 978-93-5989-528-4

Cover design: Tahira
Typesetting: Tanya Raj Upadhyay

First Edition: May 2024

Acknowledgements

With a grateful heart and humble soul,
I acknowledge those who played a role,
In shaping my journey, to this day,
And made it a remarkable way.
Firstly, to my parents, who gave me birth,
Nurtured me with love and guided me through the earth,
Their unwavering support and endless care,
Are the reasons I stand where I am, aware?
To Lord Krishna, my saviour and guide,
In Him, I found strength and stride,
Through life's ups and downs, He led the way,
And blessed me with faith every single day.
My siblings, my partners in crime,
Our bond grew stronger with time,
They taught me to laugh, love, and share,
And inspired me to dream big and dare.
My teachers, who showed me the light,
Inspired me to soar to new heights,
Their knowledge and wisdom were a treasure,
Guiding me towards a bright future, with pleasure.
To my colleagues in the bank, who made work fun,
Together we achieved and got things done,
With their support and camaraderie, I cherish,
And without them, my journey would've been perish.
My dear friends, the pillars of my joy,
With you, every moment is a precious alloy,
Your laughter, understanding, and endless care,

Have made my life's tapestry rich and rare.
Lastly, to my readers, who chose to read my story,
And be a part of my journey, with glory,
I hope my words inspired and touched your heart,
And gave you the courage to make a fresh start.
So, with gratitude and joy in my heart,
I thank each one, who played a part,
In my life's story, from start to end,
You made it a journey, worth every bend.

Prologue
Navigating Uncharted Waters: From Dreams to Banking

When I was young, the idea of a job in banking was just a small dot on the horizon, hidden by the big hopes and dreams that danced through my mind. Like many other people who dared to dream, I set my thoughts on high goals, fueled by the idea that I could do anything. My time in college took me in a direction I didn't expect, through the complicated world of the dairy business. I didn't know at the time that this trip would set me up for a career in banking.

As I reflect on my life, I find myself tracing the complicated strands of experience that have comprised the entirety of my existence. Every twist, turn, and shift has been a brushstroke on the canvas of my life. All of these experiences have moulded the banker, leader, and guide you see now.

Born into a modest working-class family in a quaint small town, my journey unfolds as a testament to resilience, dedication, and an unyielding spirit in the intricate realm of banking. The foundations of my character were laid in the crucible of a close-knit family, emphasising the values of hard work, integrity, and perseverance in the face of challenges. Guided by the indomitable strength of my parents, their wisdom became the compass steering me toward my aspirations, instilling in me both a love for knowledge and an unwavering determination to achieve my ambitions.

My early years saw a harmonic combination of academic achievement and physical skill, producing a symphony of promise that set the stage for the extraordinary voyage that lay ahead. As I began my professional journey, possibilities beckoned, and internships acted as guiding hands, driving me into the complicated fabric of the financial world. These critical events, like strokes from a brilliant artist's brush, sparked a passion in me for the delicate dance of money.

As time went on, I set out on a journey of commitment, a trip through the confusing hallways of the banking business. People spend hours and hours trying to find the secret information that makes this world work. With each step I took, I got closer to my goal and the door of chance that was waiting for me.

I went down the hard road ahead of me with a strong will and no intention of giving up. My journey was full of bold steps and careful steps, as well as mistakes and successes. My life has been like a symphony, with notes that are both dissonant and harmonious. Each note adds to the crescendo of my life's music.

The values that my ancestors instilled in me helped me find my way through the maze-like trip. Hard work, being honest, and not giving up were the North Stars that helped me find my way. These principles, which were a part of me, helped me build my work and my personality.

As the curtains of my life go up and down, I am humbled by the many events that have made me who I am today. All of the storms that tested my strength, the trials that shaped my determination, and the victories that rewarded my hard work have left a mark that will never go away. I came out of it all with a strong belief that it's important to follow your dreams, face your fear and that the journey is just as important as the goal.

As I write these words, I am filled with the hope that my story, my journey, will give other people hope. I hope with all my heart that sharing my experiences on these pages will light a fire of ambition in other people. May my story show how important it is to follow your dreams and take on the difficulties that life gives you. Just as my past experiences have made me who I am today, I am sure that every reader and every thinker can shape their own lives through the choices and actions they make.

Contents

1. Navigating Life's Challenges: A Journey Fueled by Dreams and Determination 1
2. Life Through the Prism: Embracing Colors, Balance, and Perspective 7
3. Nurtured by Love: A Family's Journey through Warmth, Struggles, and Unwavering Support 10
4. Unveiling Small-Town Dreams: Shaped by Community and Culture...........................19
5. Exploring the World of Learning 22
6. Uncovering My True Identity.......................25
7. Embracing the Uncharted Path: A Voyage of Self-Discovery...........................49
8. Guiding Light of Compassion and Mentorship 54
9. Embracing Challenges and Forging a New Path 58
10. Guiding Lights: Rahul and Prashant..........64
11. Discovering My Passion...........................68
12. Following My Dreams 72
13. Reaching New Heights 76
14. The Ties That Bind....................................94
15. Connectedness and Community 98

16. Resilience Under Rainstorms: Navigating Life's Trials and Triumphs 103

17. The Power of Resilience and Perseverance.. 109

18. Chasing Dreams, Embracing Victories: A Symphony of Achievements 122

19. Reflections on Life Experiences 129

20. Key Lessons and Insights Gained 136

21. Personal Philosophy and Values............. 143

22. Goals and Aspirations for the Future....... 150

Navigating Life's Challenges: A Journey Fueled by Dreams and Determination

My journey began the moment I was born. It was a trip I would take for the rest of my life. My life has been a journey full of ups and downs, challenges and victories, all of which were meant to test how strong and resilient I am. Unlike those who seem to have it easy, my life has been full of changes and turns.

Like many other people, I, too, have been on the path of ups and downs. I've had times of pure happiness and times of deep sadness. I know what it's like to love someone and what it's like to lose that love. I know what it's like to win and to lose. This has helped me become the person I am now. In my book, I can't wait to tell you everything about it.

My parents worked very hard to give my sisters and me the best chances in life. I was born in a rural part of Maharashtra. It was a time full of love and laughter, and everyone felt very safe. My parents had a big impact on who I am by teaching me things like how to work hard, be honest, and respect others. These ideals have helped me a lot when I've had to deal with different problems in my life.

As a child, I was always interested in learning and had a strong desire to do so. My parents' constant support and encouragement of my goals, as well as their stimulation of my natural curiosity about the world, have had a big impact on who I am today.

My passion for studying grew as I progressed through school, and I became increasingly engaged in my studies. Academic achievement has always been very important to me since I realised how essential it might be in my life. I've faced numerous challenges and setbacks in my life, but I've never lost sight of my ultimate aim of success. Despite my difficulties, I persisted and finally achieved my objectives. As I went to school, I discovered more about myself and my role in the world. Finally, as a devoted person, my life has been defined by a hunger for knowledge, a drive to acquire new things, and a desire to never stop learning.

I've learned throughout my life that it's more important to try to become the person you want to be than to just accept yourself as you are. Where I wanted to go and how I planned to get there were more important to me than where I was at the time.

My life has not been a goal, but a journey. Ralph Waldo Emerson's words have always made sense to me. I've learned that life isn't about getting somewhere in the end. Instead, it's about the things we see and learn along the way. Every step we take and every choice we make makes us who we are today. I have learned to enjoy the ride, to be grateful for the ups and downs, and to find happiness in the present. My life has been a beautiful journey so far, and I can't wait to see where it goes next. I've learned throughout my life that the trip and the lessons we learn along the way are more important than where we end up.

I grew up in a small town in India, so I knew the limits and problems that came with where I came from. I didn't come from a wealthy family, so I had to work very hard to get where I am today. But I've never let my humble beginnings stop me from getting ahead. Instead, I focused on my most important goals and the ways I could reach them in my life.

Rumi, a great poet and philosopher, once said, "Yesterday I was smart, so I wanted to change the world." As a person, this has always been one of my best statements about the topic at hand. I made some changes after I learned something new. I've learned over the course of my life how important it is to keep a good attitude in order to succeed at anything. As the saying goes, "mind over matter" is true when you're facing problems or problems. I've learned that if I keep my mind clear and focused, I can get through any problem and reach my goals. This lesson has helped me reach many of my goals and has been very important to me.

Living the life of your dreams has always struck me as the most thrilling thing you can do. This quotation is significant to me because it demonstrates that everyone, regardless of where they come from or what they are going through, has the ability to create the life they choose. When I think about my life, I remember what the great author Mirza Ghalib said: "Tell me in one sentence what you are like." These words will stay with me throughout my life, making me always wonder who I am and what I'm here for. I'm sure that what makes us who we are shouldn't be our genes or where we come from, but rather our ability to connect with others and build important relationships. This philosophy has been an important part of my life and has helped me be successful in both my personal and work life.

I've had to deal with a lot of challenges and issues throughout my life. But I've never lost sight of my dreams and goals. Over the course of my life, I've realised that true success and pleasure stem from the journey and the impact we make on the lives of those we encounter. One trip in particular jumps out in my memory as evidence of this.

As a person, I've come to understand that where I go in life is more important than who I am. My dreams and goals have shaped who I am and what I want to do with my life. I have kept in mind the wise words of Emerson, Rumi, Oprah, and Ghalib all my life. These words have helped me through the twists and turns of life by reminding me that the trip is more important than the destination.

Growing up in a small town, where most people believed that in order to achieve success, you had to be born into riches or luxury. I had always considered that such a restricted perspective was incorrect. I thought I could do anything if I worked hard, paid attention, and had a strong desire to achieve. This idea guided me throughout my life, motivating me to strive hard and passionately towards my objectives. I've always been moved by what the late, great Bob Marley said. He thought that a person's true greatness is not measured by how much money they have, but by how honest they are and how much good they can do for others. I've lived my whole life by this philosophy, and I try to show these beliefs in everything I do. I've learnt that our impact on the world is far more significant than our wealth or social standing. As the saying goes, what really counts is not what we have but what we do with it. This belief has helped me with everything in my life, from my personal ties to my work. I try to make a positive change in the lives of the people around me because I know that this is the legacy that really matters.

Thomas Edison, a great inventor, once said, "Many of life's failures are people who didn't realise how close they were to success when they gave up." I've learned over the course of my life that the only way to reach our goals is to never give up, no matter how hard the path may seem. We can get past any problem and meet our goals if we are strong-willed and don't give up. I think that to be successful, we often have to push ourselves past our limits and keep going even when we don't want to. This saying has helped me stay focused on my goals and never lose sight of what I want to accomplish.

I've learnt from my humble beginnings that striving for the heavens may lead to great things. If I put in the time, and work, and have self-control, I can achieve any goal I set for myself. Even when things didn't go as planned, I never gave up on my dreams.

Balance, and Perspective

I was always curious about how prisms could bend light and make a beautiful variety of colours. This thing about prisms has always caught my eye and made me want to know more. My life has been shaped by both good and bad things I've done. The things that have happened to me and helped me learn have made me who I am today. I've been through a lot of things in my life that have helped me become the person I am today. Like the bright colours of a prism, each of these events has added a new colour to the fabric of my life.

Like a prism, I can look back at life and refract the events that have made me who I am. As a person, I have always thought that being honest and sincere is the key to a happy life. I think of these traits as the colours of a rainbow. Each one is different and important in its own way. I've tried my whole life to show these traits in everything I do, whether it's with friends or at work. I think I can make a useful and rewarding life for myself if I stay true to myself and am honest with other people. Since I was a kid, I've always thought it was important to be honest and real. I've found that when I'm honest with myself and the people around me, I can make a real difference in society and the world. This belief has helped me with everything in my life, from my personal ties to my work. I'm thankful for the chances I've had to make a good difference, and I'm excited to keep living my life with honesty and purpose.

I've come to understand that the quality of balance that the prism shows is also a big part of my own life. I understand that I have always thought balance was important. Just like a prism needs balance to make a beautiful rainbow of colours, I've found that balance is important for a happy, successful life. Keeping my personal and professional lives, as well as my mental and physical health, in balance has been a challenge for me throughout my life. I've learned over the course of my life that the key to success and happiness is to find a balance between things that are at odds with each other. I've been able to do well in all parts of my life by finding a balance between these two extremes.

Last but not least, I learned the value of seeing things from multiple perspectives. As a young student, I was fascinated by prisms' ability to split light into its many hues dependent on the angle from which it entered. My surroundings and worldview moulded my outlook on life in the same manner. I've discovered that if you have a growth mentality, you can convert negative experiences into opportunities to learn and improve.

Subsequently, my life may be compared to a prism, which is a nice metaphor. I've seen things from many various perspectives throughout my life, such as how a prism bends light. As I reflect on all I've done and learnt, I realise how magnificent and difficult life is. Accepting these characteristics has aided me in becoming the person I am today. I've had the good fortune to see many distinct hues throughout my life, much like a prism. I'm grateful for these experiences and what they've taught me.

Nurtured by Love: A Family's Journey through Warmth, Struggles, and Unwavering Support

I grew up in a place that was full of warmth, love, and happiness. I am the youngest of four children. I was born to my parents in a small town in Maharashtra. When I was a kid, my parents worked hard to make sure our family had everything we needed. Their steadfast love and commitment made my home a warm and safe place where I could grow.

As a child, I loved spending time with my family, and I still remember those times fondly. As a kid, my family and I liked to get together for picnics at places we had never been before. My parents taught me and my sisters how important family is from the time we were young. They taught us that our happiness and success in life depended on how much we helped and cared for each other.

My parents had a major influence on who I am now when I was younger. My father, who worked for the Government Insurance Company, and mother, who was a stay-at-home mom, both motivated me to learn and instilled in me a lifelong passion for learning new things. My parents instilled in me the importance of education as I grew up. They constantly reminded my sisters and me that we should always strive our hardest in school. My parents used to buy my sisters and me a lot of tiny storybooks when we were kids. We'd be fascinated by the pages for hours, eager to absorb everything from the words to the visuals. In my story, I have to admit that I had both good and bad things happen to me when I was growing up. As a child, I was so shy that it was hard for me to make friends. My parents have always been there for me and helped me figure out how to deal with the problems I've faced. Their love and support have been very important in helping me get through hard times. I was pushed to accept myself and be proud of who I am.

Throughout my youth, my parents did everything they could to love and support my sisters and me. They worked hard to keep getting along with each other and made sure I could spend quality time with both of them.

My father has always been my motivation, constant support, and leader. I've been lucky to have someone in my life who has always been there for me no matter what. This person has always been there to help me and has given me constant support and guidance. Love, knowledge, and support have helped me become the person I am now. I am the rock that my family stands on.

As a kid, I always thought my dad looked tough. But as I got older, I understood that he really cared about his kids. Even though he sometimes seem cold and detached, he really used to care about my family and close friends. He was there for them when they needed help, comfort, or support. My father has always been a man who doesn't say much, but what he does say is worth a lot. Because of everything he has done for our family, I am proud to say that my dad is my hero. Someday, I hope to tell him how much I appreciate all the love, help, and support he has given us. Father, you are my backbone and my strength.

Through thick and thin,
you've been with me at length
Your tough exterior belies a heart of gold
With wisdom and guidance,
you've helped me unfold
Through your actions and your words,
you've taught me the right
To work hard, be disciplined,
and persevere with might
You've shown me what it means
to be a family man
To love, to care, to be there whenever you can
Your quiet strength and unwavering resolve
Have helped us through times when
problems revolve
You've never given up, you've never backed down

Your support and love has
been our constant crown

I can't help but think of my dad when I think about my life. He has been my rock, my compass, and my source of motivation. I looked up to him as a role model when I was young, and I learned so much from his knowledge and advice. He taught me the importance of working hard, not giving up, and being determined, which has helped me get through many tough times in life. I will always be thankful for his love and support, and every day I try to make him happy. As a little kid, I always wanted to fly through the air. I would look up at the birds and feel jealous, wishing that I, too, could fly. Even when things were at their worst, it helped me to know that I wasn't alone. Dad, you have always been my rock and the base of my life as my father. Your constant love and support have given me a feeling of safety and comfort that I've always loved. You have been with me through every success and failure, giving me advice and support along the way. You make me feel warm and at home in a way that I can't find anywhere else. I'm thankful for the life you've given me and the moments we've made together.

As I learn more about my background, I can't help but reflect on how much my mother influenced me. My mother's continual presence in my life made an unforgettable imprint on me. Her calm strength, loving care, and the wonderful times we spent shape my recollections of her.

With the pleasant days of my youth, she has always been the heart of our family path, I recognise that her strength and dedication are still the things that keep me going. My mother has always been the glue that held my sisters and me together.

As one of four kids, I was lucky to have a mother who handled the challenges in a family with great poise and ease. Even when things were hard, she kept going, no matter what stood in her way, she always found a way to pick herself back up and keep going. And she did all of it with a happy attitude and a lot of kindness.

When I think about what my mother did for me, I understand how much I owe her. I've been lucky enough to have a reflection who inspired me, a guide who showed me the way, and a confidant who was my best friend throughout my life. I wouldn't be the person I am today if she hadn't always loved me and pushed me forward.

So, I'm thankful for my kind mother. Since she is the heart of my family, I feel very lucky to be a part of it.

Mother, your love is like a warm embrace,
A light that shines on through the darkest days.
You've been our rock, our guiding star,
A constant presence, no matter where we are.
You've sacrificed so much to help us grow,
And taught us everything we need to know.
Your kindness, patience, and strength of will,

Have inspired us to be our best selves still.
We cherish the memories we've shared with you,
And know that your love will always shine through.
No matter where we go, or what we do,
Our hearts will always belong to you.

I owe so much to my mother for the love and support she has given me without condition. It's hard to explain how much she cares about me. And I was grateful for her constant help.

My loved ones have been my rock through all the ups and downs of my life. Having wonderful parents and three lovely sisters to grow up with has been one of the best things in my life. As a child, my father told me that being honest, working hard, and being committed are all important. These lessons have stuck with me my whole life and helped me become the person I am now. My mother is great, and she has always put the well-being of our family first. She doesn't care about herself and has given up a lot for us.

My upbringing was marked by the presence of three sisters. One of the most essential lessons I've learned is the value of collaboration, empathy, and finding a middle ground. Based on my own experiences, I've discovered that these characteristics are essential for building solid connections and excelling in both personal and professional circumstances. Throughout my life, I've been involved in several conflicts and battles..

My sisters were the driving force behind my decision to attend college and begin a professional career. My sisters are constantly thinking of innovative ways to accomplish things at work, which has always amazed me. If it weren't for my sweetness and innocence, I'd be the worst of us all. It's hard for me to find the right words to describe how important my sisters are to me. I've been lucky to have sisters who have stuck by me through every struggle and success in my life. Their steady support has given me strength and comfort, and I know I can count on them to always have my back, no matter what.

As kids, we were always together. I remember the times when I had the most fun and when I was closest to other people. These were the times when we worked together to solve problems and came out on top. Through these things we did together, we became closer and learned a lot about each other. Our friendship got stronger as time went on. We've been through the ups and downs of life together, always there to calm and support each other.

When I'm sad, my sisters are the first people I turn to. As a person. I've been lucky to have sisters in my life who were always there for me when I needed help. They were always ready to listen when I needed to talk to someone, and they always knew how to cheer me up when I was sad.

At different times in my life, I've felt like the weight of the world was on my shoulders. My sisters have been my steady companions my whole life. When things were hard, they gave me the comfort and support I needed. Their steady presence has given me strength and reminded me that I'm never really alone, even when things look the worst. I've learned that life isn't always a smooth ride as I've gone through it. But I've come to see that despite the problems, we're still tied together.

I love my sisters and the bond we have with each other. I wouldn't be the person I am today if it weren't for them. They were very important to my growth and progress as a person. When I think about my life, I am excited about everything that has happened and everything that will happen. I am sure that I can get through any problem that comes my way, especially with the help of my family and friends. Together, we've been through a lot of tough times and always come out on top.

Sisters, shoulder to shoulder we stand,
Together through thick and thin, hand in hand,
Fighting, loving, crying, living life,
Navigating the highs and lows of strife.
You're my rock, my confidant, my friend,
Our bond was unbreakable until the very end,
In your embrace, I find solace and peace,
Your love and support will never cease.
Through the storms of life, we hold fast,
With you by my side, I can face anything at last,

Sisters, you mean the world to me,
Forever together, we'll always be

My family has been there for me through all of life's ups and downs and has always been a source of support and strength. When it was hard for me to find work, my parents gave me the drive to keep looking for work. I got through the worst times in my life because I never lost faith in myself. When I was sad, I always went to my sisters for support and a dose of reality.

I will always be grateful to my family for the help they have given me throughout my life. Whenever I ran into a problem in my life, I always turned to my family for help and support. Even now, this is still true. I'm thankful for the people in my life who have always been there for me. Their support has been the pushing force behind everything I've done.

Ultimately my family has had the greatest influence on my development. I will never forget all of their assistance and wisdom in shaping me into the person I am today.

When I reflect back on my childhood, I am grateful for how much my family always loved and supported me. The groundwork was laid for me to become the person I am today. Ethics and ideals instilled in me as a youngster have guided me throughout my life. I've always had a lot of regard for my youth and the people that influenced my growth and development.

Unveiling Small-Town Dreams: Shaped by Community and Culture

I was born and raised in a small town in Maharashtra called Shahada. It is in the Nandurbar district. Growing up in this town gave me a special experience that helped me become the person I am now. As I grew up, I was surrounded by indigenous people who called this place home. I grew up in Shahada, which is a small town with few resources, but it has its own special beauty.

I was always impressed by how strong the sense of community was at the house where I grew up. As a youngster, I was fortunate to grow up in a place with a strong feeling of community. People who lived there were extremely familiar with one another, and there was a lot of mutual respect in the way we spoke to one another. This created a welcoming and helpful environment in which everyone felt like they belonged and were respected. During festivities, I noted that individuals from all origins would gather to participate in various rituals and consume the region's unique dishes. As I grew up in that town, I couldn't help but notice how the presence of the local indigenous people gave it its own unique character. Everywhere I looked, I saw different foods, ways of dressing, and ways of living. It was incredible to see how each person has their own traditions and ways of doing things. I understood that we can all be more tolerant and accepting of each other if we understand and value our different cultures. Since I was young, the culture of the people around me has always interested me. I've always been struck by how close they are to the land, and I've always thought that was a great thing.

It was good and bad to grow up in a small place. Even though the area was beautiful and had a lot of culture, there were some bad things about living in such a small town. I remember that infrastructure and budget problems caused me a lot of trouble. These problems stopped me from reaching my goals and dreams in a big way. It was hard to grow up in a place where there wasn't much infrastructure. Few people had easy access to things like hospitals, schools, and roads. I've had to deal with a lot of problems that have made it hard for me to take advantage of certain opportunities or use resources that were there.

Even though we didn't have much, we were able to get by and do well. As I got older, I liked the simplicity and beauty of where I was born more and more. Growing up in a quiet place with little noise pollution helped me pay attention to the important people and relationships in my life.

The unique beauty and charm of my town always drew me in. I felt a strong sense of duty to share its culture and customs with the rest of the world. This made me want to promote and celebrate the unique things about my place around the world.

In the past few years, I've seen new roads, schools, and hospitals being built in my town, which is a clear sign of growth. I've always been proud of my hometown's unique personality and how well its people and surroundings get along. I hope that as the town changes and gets better, it will still keep its own character and be a place where everyone can live together in peace.

Exploring the World of Learning

The streets of Shahada, a small town in northern Maharashtra, India, where I grew up, were warmed by the sun. Here, in the colourful tapestry of different people's lives and countries, I started to learn about myself and grow. Since I was a young child, the colourful sights, sounds, and smells of this community have left a lasting mark on my impressionable mind, giving me a deep appreciation for how different people are.

As I started my journey through school, the doors of a simple basic school opened to let me in. Inside its small walls, I found not only a place to learn but also a sanctuary of information that would help me get started in school. Among the many great people who helped me, Shri Rajbhoj sir stands out. On my first day, he met me with a warm smile. He was tall and kind, and his smile set the tone for a journey of learning and discovery.

Over time, my admiration and affection for Shri Rajbhoj sir grew immensely. He wasn't just a teacher; he played multiple roles as a leader, a friend, and a guide. His unwavering belief in our potential fueled our determination and motivated us to aim for greatness. Reflecting on my journey, I realize how profoundly he influenced my perspective on learning and personal growth.

Shri Rajbhoj sir imparted lessons that extended far beyond the confines of the classroom. He instilled in me the significance of kindness and compassion, values that have been invaluable throughout my life. His efforts to support and uplift his students inspired me to adopt a similar approach in my teaching. Empathy and positive encouragement have become the cornerstone of my teaching style, kindling a sense of promise in each student I encounter.

The lessons of two very special people—my father and Shri Rajbhoj sir—are woven into the fabric of my life. I learned to be committed, disciplined, and persistent from my father. On the other hand, my teacher helped me believe in myself and my skills. He taught me that my dreams had no limits and that if I worked hard, I could do great things.

As I went through the different parts of my life, I realised that the small school in Shahada was a big part of my story. There, I met teachers who blew my mind, classmates who were just like me, and people who helped me figure out what I wanted to be like. Shri Rajbhoj sir was at the centre of it all. He was an original innovator in education who sparked my interest and made me want to learn more. His lessons became the guide star that showed me how to reach my goals.

From the time I was very young, I was inspired to learn, and that fire still burns strongly in me today. The information I learned from my early teachers was the foundation on which I built my sense of self.

Shri Rajbhoj sir's unbreakable spirit, the town of Shahada, the school, and the things I learned there taught me to be kind, work hard, and believe in everyone's potential. Their impact stays with me, like the steady flow of a river, as I go through the twists and turns of life. As I write down these memories, I am aware of how much these events have shaped who I am today. I am the result of the rich soil where the seeds of knowledge were planted.

Uncovering My True Identity

Going through a lot of changes, I went on a deep trip of self-discovery to find out who I really was. This part of my life tells about the steps I took to find my way through the maze of my beliefs, ideas, and goals and come out the other side with a new sense of self-awareness that would shape my future.

When I embarked on this path of self-reflection, I went deep into soul-searching, peeling back the layers of my existence. My big and subtle events spread before me like a tapestry, demonstrating the delicate interaction that moulded me. Aside from reflecting on my heritage, I also reflected on my future hopes and goals.

Upon deeper inspection, I identified several factors that led to my development. The town of Shahada, which was packed with various people and vivid life, shaped the ideals that now form the cornerstone of my views. The busy streets were a canvas on which each individual I met contributed a distinctive brushstroke to my growing knowledge. This melting pot's rich tapestry of diverse cities, religions, and experiences created a strong appreciation for variety.

During this process of self-discovery, I realised that not all of my thoughts and views were fundamentally mine. The outside world had inadvertently formed my psyche, imprinting beliefs and assumptions that I had unknowingly embraced. Armed with this knowledge, I set out to reclaim my story, peel back the layers of influence and fear, and recover the heart of my genuine self.

The trip was not without difficulties. Writing my book exposed me, forcing me to reveal the intricacies of my life for all to see. Maintaining authenticity became my guiding principle, grounding me in my values in the face of cultural changes. This fortitude enabled me to carve my own path without apology, delving into uncharted territory in my search for authentic self-expression.

Integral to this narrative is the imprint left by Shri Rajbhoj Sir, my initial mentor on this odyssey of self-discovery. As I commenced my formal education, his kind and luminous face illuminated my way. The classroom, a space of learning, transformed into a haven where he imparted wisdom and guidance. His counsel taught me that honesty was not just a virtue but also a beacon illuminating the path to true self-realisation.

My connection to the earth and the realm of agriculture remained steadfast, even amid the academic corridors where familial expectations and personal goals converged. Struggling with these conflicting forces, I found myself at an unexpected crossroads. Choosing a different path aligned with my passion for dairy science, where my spirit felt at home and thrived.

This transformative journey marked a significant chapter in my life, unravelling layers and helping me ascertain my true identity. It underscores the resilience of the human spirit, the importance of authenticity, and the liberating nature of embracing oneself. Through struggles, triumphs, pursuit of interests, and mentorship, I continued to learn more about who I am, a journey that will persist in shaping the chapters yet to unfold.

I began a journey of self-discovery, Iand had a strong urge to learn more about my views and values.

Step one on my road was to look inside myself. As I thought about my life up to that point, I couldn't help but think about how my events had made me who I am today. I also thought about what I wanted to do to make my hopes and dreams come true. As I learned more about my own life, I realised that a lot of different things had led to my growth as a person. I understand that my childhood and culture have had a big impact on how I think and feel. When I was growing up, I was surrounded by a variety of family members, friends, and people from the community who all helped me learn about the world. Through these things, I've learned how important variety is and how valuable different points of view are. During my journey of self-discovery, I learned how important it was to recognise and question how other people's thoughts and views affected me. As I started my own journey, I started to think about myself and look at my own views and values. I questioned the ideas and expectations that had been put on me.

Writing my book wasn't easy, and I ran into some resistance and pushback along the way. As I got older, I realised that being true to myself was essential to having a happy life. Even if my ideals and beliefs were different from those around me, it was important to me to stay true to them. I knew that if I wanted to be honest, I had to stick to my own set of rules, no matter how strange they might have seemed.

By going through this process, I learned more about my core values and principles. I have a deep respect for social fairness and equality because of what I have been through. I notice that I have always put the most value on being real and honest. Also, I've always thought it was very important to be true to yourself and show who you are. My journey of self-reflection hasn't been a one-time thing. From what I've learned, my identity is not something easy that can be summed up in a single word or idea.

When I think about my life, I'm thankful for the challenges and successes and the ideals that guide me. I'm thankful for the chances I've had to grow and learn about myself. I'm looking forward to the next steps on this road, and I'm grateful to the people and situations that have helped me along the way.

My educational journey began at Gagarani classes in my hometown of Shahada during my junior college years. Mr. Gagarani, a dedicated teacher who saw great potential in each student, became my mentor. Despite my initial lack of interest in medicine, my father, always passionate about my education, encouraged me to pursue a medical career.

Initially, I was hesitant, uncertain about becoming a doctor, and lacking enthusiasm for studying medicine. However, my deep-rooted faith led me to trust in Mr. Gagarani's expertise. Despite my reservations, I decided to give it a try. Surprisingly, I performed well in the first trial test for medical school admission.

Upon winning the mock test, I could sense Mr. Gagarani's happiness. Convinced of my potential, he urged me to pursue a medical career. Despite my success in the practice test, I found my true interest in dairy science. This passion led me to gain valuable experience and knowledge in the fields of agriculture and dairy products. Instead of opting for medical school, I chose a path aligned with my genuine interests.

While Mr. Gagarani initially seemed disappointed, he eventually understood and accepted my perspective. It dawned on me that I possessed various hobbies and passions, and it was crucial to carve my own path in life.

I deeply appreciate Mr. Gagarani's support, realising how fortunate I was to have someone who believed in me more than I believed in myself during my youth. This influential figure encouraged me to step out of my comfort zone and explore new opportunities. With his guidance, I began to recognise the untapped potential within myself. Despite going against conventional wisdom, I had faith in my choices.

Choosing dairy technology as my major turned out to be a significant and fulfilling decision. Since childhood, my fascination with farms and science, coupled with the understanding that pursuing an uninteresting field would leave me unsatisfied, led me to this path. I trusted that Mr. Gagarani would appreciate my decision to follow my heart rather than conform to external expectations.

Reflecting on my life, I've learned that the pursuit of happiness is paramount. Following my hobbies and goals has always been crucial. As I grew older, my interest in dairy technology deepened, driven by a desire to contribute to improving and securing our food supply. Through hard work and commitment, I've been fortunate to excel in my pursuits. Whether working in a hospital, conducting lab research, or creating new dairy products, I strive to make a positive impact on the world.

Looking back on my accomplishments so far, I feel proud and excited about what lies ahead. I am confident that by pursuing my passions and goals, I can make a difference in the world and leave a lasting legacy for future generations. Throughout my journey, I've realised the importance of receiving help from others, as their support has been instrumental in overcoming challenges and achieving my goals.

When I was in college, those were the good old days. During that time, I changed a lot as a person, went to school learned a lot, and had a lot of fun along the way. College changed the course of my life in a big way. During this time, I met people who would stay my friends for the rest of my life and laid the groundwork for a successful career in dairy technology.

On my first day of college, I felt a mix of excitement, nervousness, and eagerness that I will never forget. I remember a time when I was eager to learn more, make new friends, and dive into the fascinating world of dairy technology. When I walked through the university's walls for the first time, I was amazed and interested. All of the unknown faces around me were excited and ready to go, just like I was.

In the first few weeks of my life, I met a lot of new people, went to a lot of new places, and did a lot of new things. When I first got to campus, I was amazed by how big it was and how many great resources were offered to students. The teachers were all experts in their areas, and I was amazed by how much they knew and how long they had been teaching. As a young person, I wanted to learn as much as possible and couldn't get enough information.

Over the course of a few weeks and months, I made a schedule that helped me balance my schoolwork, extracurricular interests, and social life. As a student, I always did my best in class and really wanted to learn.

I tried to find a good mix between schoolwork and fun things to do. Throughout my life, I've had many chances to relax, enjoy the moment, and make memories that are important to me. During my time at college, I was always in the middle of a lively, busy environment. There was never a dull time. There were festivals, games, and field trips.

I was lucky enough to meet some of my best friends. When I was in college, I was lucky to have a close group of friends who stuck by each other through good times and bad. We spent a lot of time together, whether we were studying for tests or just having fun. We knew we could always count on each other because our friendship was solid. My life has been full of amazing things, like spontaneous road trips and staying up all night to study with friends.

I had the chance to work as an intern at a dairy plant, which turned out to be one of the most rewarding things I've ever done. Getting to use what I had learned in school was the best thing I could have done. Because of what I've been through, I have a deep understanding of the problems that farms face every day. I've learned how important it is to have high moral standards and how complicated it is to run a dairy farm.

I went through a big change that changed the course of my life. It was a time when I started to feel like I was getting better and making progress on my own journey. During that time, I learned a lot about myself and grew as a person. I learned to accept both my skills and weaknesses, and I pushed myself to leave my comfort zone. As I got older, I became sure of myself and what I could do. I learned how to think for myself and took on the tasks of being an adult head-on. I left a permanent mark on the world around me because of what I did.

When I think about my time at college, I feel both thankful and nostalgic. I was lucky enough to get a great education when I was growing up, which helped me become the person I am today. Along the way, I also found a lot of ways to have fun and grow as a person. During my time there, the people I met and the things that happened to me were important parts of my successful career path in dairy science, and they will always be important to me.

As someone who has been to college, I have some simple tips for people who are just starting out: have fun, learn as much as you can, and make thc most of every moment. During my time in college, I had experiences that I will remember for the rest of my life., I understand I've always been willing to try new things and take risks. I'm sure that life gives us many chances, and it's up to us to take advantage of them. This way of thinking has taken me on many adventures and let me do things I never thought I could do. I want everyone to try new things and enjoy everything that life has to offer.

Dr. Madhav Patil, who was my professor while I was at Pusad, was a very nice person. I knew right away that he was someone special who would have a big effect on my life.

Dr. Patil first caught my attention because of his impressive background and achievements in dairy science. He knew everything there was to know about the subject and could explain even the most complicated ideas. His ability to break down complicated ideas has helped others. He always tried to make learning easy and clear for students. It makes me happy that the students he's taught will remember what he's done for a long time.

As I got to know Dr. Patil better, I started to like him as a person, not just for what he had done in college. I know a lot about what it means to be human. As a follower of Krishna, I began to see Dr. Patil as a manifestation of God. He is really good at getting his students to push themselves to their limits, do their best, and never give up on their goals. Dr. Patil has always been there for me, which is something I'm very grateful for whether it was with my college work or with personal problems.

Dr. Patil had a big impact on my life because he taught me how important it is to keep trying and work hard. This lesson has become a cornerstone of my personal outlook and has helped me succeed in many areas of my life. My dad taught me that it's important to work hard and keep going even when things get hard. I learned at a young age that success isn't just about being smart, but also about working hard and not giving up. I was taught these beliefs, and they have changed how I deal with problems and work towards my goals.

I was able to do a lot and learn a lot during my time in Pusad because he taught me. As a student, I was always serious and careful, and I always did my best in everything I did. Dr. Patil was there for me every step of the way. He always told me to aim for excellence and never give up.

Dr. Patil gave me a new way of seeing things, which I think is one of the best things I've ever gotten. When I think about my life, I think about the person who taught me what it means to really live. He showed me that success and getting things are not the only things that matter in life. He showed me instead that the point of life is to find something greater and more important.

Thanks to the lessons I learned and the help I got, I learned to enjoy digging into life's philosophical foundations. I realise that I have learned to value every situation, even the ones that were hard. Through my journey, I've learned that there is always a chance for happiness and joy, even when things are hard.

Dr. Madhav Patil is a name I will never forget. He was an important part of my life, and I will always remember what he did for me. Because of him, the way my life went changed. He wasn't just a teacher; he was also a friend, a guide, and a leader. I had never met anyone with my charm and unique personality. He made me feel better.

He knew plenty, about various things and shared information in a unique way. He would use examples and stories from real life to get their attention and help them understand what he was talking about. He knew a lot about the subject and always made sure his students understood the basics.

Dr. Madhav Patil has always been the kind of teacher who pushes his students to do their best. He made me believe that if I work hard, I can get what I want. He would often tell me that there are no fast cuts to success and that you have to work hard to get there. His words have stuck with me my whole life and have always pushed me to do my best. He thinks that a person's moral principles and values are just as important as their intelligence when it comes to figuring out their total value.

Dr. Madhav Patil has taught me a lot and helped me a lot. I am grateful to him for that. I owe a lot of my personal growth and character development to him because he was a big part of making me who I am today. He was more to me than just a teacher. I will never forget the things taught me, and I will always be grateful for the chance to have learned from him.

There was an event that I still remember very well. Unfortunately, I forgot to turn in my dairy chemistry assignment work the day before the practice test. As I sat in the testing room, the idea of having to go back to my room to get the task made me feel sick. I was worried that I might be late for the test and lose points because of it.

As I walked back to my room to get my homework, I couldn't help but think about all the fights I'd been in. Throughout my life, I've had times when I forgot important information, made mistakes, or ran into problems I wasn't expecting. As for me, what makes me different is how I deal with hard times.

Dr. Madhav Patil was keeping track of the homework when I got back to the lab. When I saw that a few of my classmates had come back to turn in their work, I told them to finish up and come with me to the test. Even though the steps made perfect sense, I felt like I couldn't handle what was going on. What happened next would make me think about it for a long time.

As I was getting ready to start my practical test, Dr. Patil came up to me to see how I was doing. At first, I was shocked by how kind he was. After all, he was known as a tough teacher who wouldn't put up with any crap. As my talk with him went on, though, I realised how much he cared about me. I understood how serious the situation was and was worried about their safety as a result. I was lucky to have Dr. Patil's care and support when I was in a tough position. Maya Angelou said that people will never forget how you make them feel, which made me think of what he did. Dr. Patil's kindness and concern made me feel important and cared for, even when things were hard. It was a lesson that kindness and care can be found even in the worst of times.

I learned something important about life that day. I've learned over the course of my life that struggle is an unavoidable part of being human. But what makes us who we are is not the battle itself, but how we choose to deal with it. I've had to deal with a lot of problems in my life, but I've always tried to do so with a good attitude and a strong will to get through them. This way of thinking has helped me grow as a person and made me reach many of my goals and dreams. I think that by taking on the challenges that life gives us, we can become stronger, more resilient, and eventually more successful in all parts of our lives. I could either give in to my problems or work through them and move on. Dr. Patil's kindness and support when I was in trouble made a big difference in my life. It taught me how important kindness is and how important even the smallest acts of kindness are.

In a lot of ways, my life has been like a laboratory. I have always pushed my limits and dealt with problems I didn't expect. The key to how well my tests have turned out has always been how well I look at the data I collect. I've always thought that when we're faced with problems in life, we have a choice. We can choose to see them only as bad things, or we can choose to see them as chances to grow and learn. This point of view has been my guide throughout my life. It has helped me get past many problems and reach my goals.

"The wound is where the light enters you," is a quote by Rumi that has always made sense to me. I've had to deal with a lot of hard times and problems in my life, which have tried my strength and ability to bounce back. Even though these situations were often hard and upsetting, they also gave me chances to grow and change. I've learned that struggle can be a strong force for change and that even in the darkest times, there is always a glimmer of light waiting to shine through. I understand that my experiences have helped me grow as a learner and as a person. I've come to realise that every situation offers a lot of opportunities to learn and grow. I've learned that it's important to believe in yourself and keep going when things get hard.

I can't help but think that day in the lab was a big deal. As I've gone through life, I've learned how important it is to be patient, have understanding, and do random acts of kindness and the person whom I helped will always be appreciated.

Even after all these years, I still remember the things that happened in the microbiology lab. It was a normal day in the dairy microbiology lab, where I worked with a very strict professor named Dr. Khedkar. On one of my days, I was always feeling nervous. As I was getting ready to take a sample from the test tube, I was lucky that Dr. Khedkar was watching me closely in front of the whole class. As I started, my hands began to shake, and I became more careful about what I did. As I held the inoculating loop and the test tube, their repetitive "tin tin tin tin" seemed to make fun of me.

I was scared when Dr. Khedkar suddenly said, "Ye Mahajanaya kay karto re." The words, which in our original language meant "Hey, Mahajan, what are you doing?", sent shivers down my spine. As I stood in the empty lab, I thought about what Dr. Khedkar had said. All eyes were on me, and everyone was waiting for me to speak. As I looked at my work, I realised I was feeling anxious. Even though I tried to cool down, it was hard for me to pay attention to my work. As I looked inside me, I felt embarrassed, and my face started to get red. I just couldn't believe how silly I looked. As I sat in front of Dr. Khedkar, his strict attitude made me feel even more nervous. I was sure he would tell me off for making a mistake.

To my surprise, Dr. Khedkar smiled and waited for me to say something. But I didn't say anything, and I couldn't help but wonder what was on his mind. I could tell that he didn't yell at me because he seemed to sense that I was nervous. From that, I learned that even I, one of the strictest people I know, have a kinder side.

This reminded me of a famous quote by Franklin D. Roosevelt: "The only thing we have to fear is fear itself." I've learned over the course of my life that fear can be a crippling feeling that keeps us from reaching our goals. I had to get past my fears in order to reach my full potential.

When I think about my life, I think of a saying by Nelson Mandela that really speaks to me: "I learned that courage was not the absence of fear, but the victory over it." "A man is brave not if he never feels afraid, but if he overcomes that fear." Throughout my life, I've learned that real courage comes from being able to face and get past one's fears.

I've learned that nervousness and worry are normal parts of being human. But I've also learned that it's important not to let our feelings decide what we do and how we act. I've always thought that you should jump right into difficulties and use them as chances to grow. When I looked at the smile on Dr Khedkar's face after the event, I couldn't help but think that everyone should get a second chance.

This gave me the courage to try new things and help me get over my fear of failing. Throughout my life, I've learned that everyone, no matter how strict they seem, has a soft side. I've also learned that it's better to try and fail than to never try at all.

I learned something important from what happened to me in the microbiology lab. My life was driven by the desire to get over my fears and become the best version of myself. I've had to deal with a lot of hard things in my life, but there's one lesson that has always stuck with me and helped me get through them. As a person, I've come to understand that facing our fears is an important part of being successful in life.

I will always remember this lesson because it has given me the strength to stick with things when they get hard. I have learned over the course of my life that fear and worry are normal human reactions. But I've also learned that these feelings don't have to stop us from reaching our goals. By having the right attitude, I was able to get over my fears and be successful in many areas of my life.

When I think about my time in Pusad, I'll always be thankful for how Dr. Patil shaped me. My mentor taught me the morals and principles that have guided me throughout my whole life and gave me the skills I needed to do well in my field.

As a student, I was lucky to have Dr. Patil as a teacher. He was a very smart and inspiring teacher. I would tell anyone who has the chance to learn from a person as amazing as this to make the most of the time they have with them and always remember the important lessons they teach. As a great teacher, he always created a big impact on his students and helped them become who they really are and reach their full potential.

After I finish my Bachelor of Science in Dairy Technology, I'm excited to use the information and skills I've learned to start a new journey in the business world. I didn't know how to go about getting my Master's degree in Agri-Business Management, which was my goal. I had to choose between getting an MBA in the traditional way or looking into other possibilities.

After careful consideration and overcoming the fear of failure, I enrolled in the International Postgraduate Diploma in General Insurance at the Institute of Insurance and Risk Management (IIRM) in Hyderabad. The programme seemed tailor-made for my skills and interests, particularly my fascination with understanding and managing risks.

The course at IIRM proved to be challenging and rigorous, putting my skills to the test. Working alongside a group of bright and driven individuals, all eager to make a significant impact in the insurance industry, added a dynamic element to my learning experience. Throughout my time at IIRM, I faced demanding assignments that spanned a wide spectrum of issues, allowing me to delve deep into the intricacies of the insurance business.

The programme not only expanded my knowledge but also honed my abilities in analysing and rating risks, as well as managing underwriting and claims. Despite the difficulties, the course provided a valuable opportunity for personal and professional growth, affirming my passion for the intricate world of insurance.

I was excited to see how strong I was. I spent a lot of time learning about different things and doing very well in my classes. During my time at IIRM, I found that the teachers were very helpful and knowledgeable. They always pushed me to do my best and aim high. I got to meet other people who work in the insurance business and learn about their jobs. It was a real treat for me to pick their heads about the business. The connections I've made over the years have been very important to the success of everything I've done since.

The most important thing I learned from my time at IIRM was that I was making progress and getting better in my own life. During my time in the course, I got better at critical thinking, solving problems, and making my points clear. Throughout my life, I've had chances to improve my skills in many different ways. One of my most important accomplishments has been learning how to work well with others to reach shared goals as part of a team. I've also gotten better at managing my time, which lets me put chores in order of importance and finish them quickly.

With the help of IIRM's programme, I was able to start a successful and fulfilling job in the insurance industry. I've had the chance to work for some of India's best insurance companies because of my skills in risk management and protecting assets. My life changed a lot when I went to IIRM and got my International Post Graduate Diploma in General Insurance. When I look back, I feel a deep sense of thankfulness and satisfaction that I made that choice. The moment I made that choice was a turning point in my life. It set me on a road that led to new experiences and chances I never would have imagined.

My life has been guided by the idea that I should trust my gut, take some risks, and do what I love. That's the advice I'd give to anyone in a similar position. I've always thought that life is too short to be happy with just average things. Because of this idea, I always try to do my best in everything I do. I always try to be the best version of myself, whether it's in my personal or work life. I don't want to waste my time on things that don't make me happy or help me grow. This way of thinking has given me a lot of great chances and experiences, and I'm thankful for every step I've taken towards my goals. I've always looked for new adventures and chances, and I've never been afraid to go down roads that aren't as popular. When I was young, I had no idea where life would take me. Many things could happen in the future. As I got older, I learned to be open to what I didn't know and to take chances. Every choice I made took me in a different direction, and I never knew where it would take me. But I trusted my gut and went with my heart, which led me on a journey I could never have imagined.

During my time at IIRM Hyderabad, I had the privilege of meeting two individuals, Rahul and Prashant, who became instrumental in shaping my outlook on life. Living with Rahul, a close friend with unwavering values centred around honesty and groundedness, provided me with invaluable insights.

Rahul's clear vision and commitment to excellence in both academics and his professional pursuits served as constant inspiration. His fearless approach to problems, coupled with creative problem-solving, showcased his determination. Rahul's authentic and honest perspective on life fostered a strong bond between us, making him a trusted friend and confidant.

In contrast, Prashant, a deeply religious and sensitive person, introduced me to the transformative power of spiritual practices. His immersion in meditation and heightened awareness opened up new realms of possibilities for personal growth. Intrigued by Prashant's profound worldview, I found myself eager to delve deeper into the teachings he shared.

Both Rahul and Prashant played pivotal roles in my life. Rahul's lessons instilled in me a realistic and practical approach to problem-solving, emphasising the importance of taking charge of my own achievements. On the other hand, Prashant's teachings on meditation and awareness equipped me with tools to navigate anxiety and find inner peace.

Their influences prompted me to reassess my existing beliefs, contemplate alternative perspectives, and embrace the inevitable uncertainties and changes in life. I am grateful for their guidance during my time at IIRM Hyderabad. I credit them for helping me overcome the challenges of adapting to a new environment and charting my own path.

Having such influential figures in my life taught me essential lessons, one of the most significant being the importance of embracing one's flaws while striving to lead a life filled with meaning and passion. Rahul and Prashant are among the fortunate individuals who have left a lasting impact on my journey. I have cherished their company, sought their advice, and never taken our friendship for granted. Reflecting on my life, I recognise that the people I've met and the relationships I've formed have significantly shaped the person I've become. These experiences have propelled me towards realising my full potential and embracing the person I am today.

Embracing the Uncharted Path: A Voyage of Self-Discovery

I was at a fork in the road in my life. It was a time when I chose to go on a journey of self-discovery to learn more about who I really was and what I was here to do. I started out on this unknown path with a heart full of curiosity and a mind open to new encounters.

My life took a big turn when I went from being a teenager to a young adult. It was a time of a lot of change, and I decided to go in a different direction. I was looking for myself and for real happiness. In this fascinating part of my life's journey, I skillfully weave together the threads of my many different experiences. I bravely step into the unknown waters of ambiguity, boldly take charge of my own fate, and fully embrace the enlightenment that comes with making my own way.

I found myself at a crossroads in my life where I had to make a big decision. Society's standards and my own goals were both pulling me in different directions.

As soon as I understood what was going on, I set out on a deep journey of self-discovery. I realised that the only way to really find myself was to get up the courage to follow my dreams and interests with all my heart. Self-doubt got in the way of what I could have done until someone told me they believed in me. Their unwavering faith gave me a spark that pushed me out of my comfort zone and into the uncharted land of authenticity.

I was determined to go against the constant stream of uniformity that was trying to swallow me up. Instead, I fully accepted the depths of my own natural tendencies, without apologising and without any doubts. When I decided to specialise in dairy science, my life took a really exciting turn. It was an area that brought together my interests in science and farming. Every step I took brought me deeper into the fascinating world of agriculture. It was a road that fit with the very core of who I am and made me want to learn more than anything else.

In my relentless pursuit of my interests, I found that I was digging deep into an endless source of happiness and meaning. When I think about my life as a whole, I keep coming back to a story that happened when I was in college. It was a time of great change when the seeds of personal growth and educational enlightenment were planted. In the end, it left an indelible mark on my life. I could feel an electric energy in the air as soon as I stepped onto campus. It was a mix of joy and worry that I would never forget.

When I think about my trip, I am reminded of the university, which is a holy place full of knowledge and opportunities. I found myself in a world of intellectual curiosity and deep self-discovery inside the hallowed halls of this prestigious university. My never-ending desire to learn was fed by the university, which gave me the chance to dig deep into the academic world and beyond. From the start, I was drawn to the way my friends got along with each other. It felt like we were all on the same trip, brought together by our desire to learn and grow. The intelligence of the professors only made me want to learn more. Their knowledge and hard work really inspired me and pushed me to hit new academic heights. But it wasn't just the people I met that made my schooling so special. I couldn't believe how many tools I had at my disposal. From well-stocked libraries to labs with the latest technology, I could learn and explore anything. This wide range of tools and chances to learn only made me want to learn more. When I think about those years, I'm thankful for the things that changed me. Friendship, talent, and a never-ending supply of resources all played a role. During my time in college, I was always engaged in a world where theory and practice fit together perfectly. I always tried to bridge the gap between the classroom and the lab, whether I was listening to a lesson or doing an experiment with my own hands. I had no idea at the time that this goal would change my career path in ways I could never have imagined.

In the middle of my academic journey, I found myself in a delicate mix between learning new things and enjoying free time. These two parts of my life fit together perfectly, producing a beautiful symphony where my academic work and my favourite free time danced together. Immersed in the mix of college life, I had to find my way through a world of hard classes and exciting parties. During this time, I had the chance to build strong, lasting relationships with other people. These ties became strong pillars of support that gave me comfort and strength as the waves of life changed.

As I start to think about myself, the pages of my life story open up in front of me. In these parts, I come to a deep realisation: there is an undeniable link between authenticity, passion, and happiness. With the advice that the respected Mr. Gagarani gave me, I set out on a journey that would change me and eventually lead me to a road that was woven into the very fabric of my being. As soon as I decided to start my journey into the world of dairy technology, something inside of me lit up. It was like a spark had been lit, showing a clear way forward that would have a big effect.

In my never-ending search for joy and authenticity, I set out on a trip that showed me how deeply beautiful it is to embrace one's passions and beliefs. My identity started to take shape as each experience, friendship, and moment in the hallowed halls of academia added to it. I start this amazing journey with a heart full of joy and a deep sense of purpose. Every step I take is a sign of how powerful it is to be my true, authentic self.

I will talk in-depth about how much I changed Dr. Madhav Patil's life. As an account, it's important to think about how I affected the people I met, and Dr. Patil's story is one that rings true.

My life is like a complicated patchwork, but there is a bright thread that runs through the whole thing. This thread is none other than Dr. Madhav Patil, a remarkable person whose deep influence has left an indelible mark on the canvas of my personal journey. As a teacher and a friend, their advice and care were crucial in showing me the way and, in the end, changing the course of my life.

Dr. Madhav Patil, a great person who was more than just an educator, helped me along my path. His impact on my life went far beyond the classroom, as he became a source of knowledge and kindness. Through his lessons, he not only made me smarter but also helped me become the person I am today. Under his guidance , I went on a life-changing trip that showed me the deep connection between always striving for excellence and the basic values of persistence and hard work. My own father had taught me these very same values, which formed the core of my character. The strong pillars on which I built my dreams were the foundations I had put in place. They were my guide light and helped me get through the many hard times and happy times that lay ahead.

I talked about how his guidance helped me build strong relationships that went far beyond the classroom. One of these important connections was with Dr. Patil. He showed that teaching is more than just sharing information; it can also be about making friends and having understanding. His unwavering positivity in the face of trouble has always shown that a positive attitude and a determined spirit can overcome any problem.

I have a powerful memory that has stuck with me for a long time. It shows that Dr. Patil was always there for me when things were hard. I was in the middle of a practical test when I found myself in a tough situation. On the one hand, I had done my homework carefully and was eager to hand it in so it could be graded. On the other hand, I was very aware of how important it was to be on time and to stick to the time range that had been set. During this time of uncertainty, I was lucky enough to meet Dr. Patil, a unique person whose caring personality and wise advice would leave an indelible mark on my life. Dr. Patil came to me in a gentle manner and a real concern for my well-being. At this crucial time, Dr. Patil's words hit me deeply and gave me the understanding and reassurance I needed so badly. Their caring attitude and knowledge of my situation gave me a new sense of calm and confidence that helped me get through the situation. I learned that people have an amazing ability to remember not only what you say or do, but also how you make them feel, even when they are having a hard time or facing problems.

When I think back on the amazing journey of my life, I can't help but feel an overwhelming sense of gratitude for the amazing chance meeting I had with Dr. Madhav Patil, which was a gift from fate. I was lucky enough to meet a remarkable mentor whose advice turned out to be a priceless gift. Outside of education, this person's impact was far-reaching and left a lasting mark on my life. I became the person I am today because of what he taught me about how important it is to be kind, have understanding, and be strong. Dr. Patil had a huge effect on my character and personal growth. He helped me become the person I am today.

His advice changed me from the inside out, making me a person who not only wanted to learn but also showed love and care. As I deal with the difficulties of life, I find comfort in the things I've learned. These lessons are a steady reminder that real success is more than just getting things done.

It's not just about how many awards we get, but also about how much we change the lives of the people around us.

In the pages of my story, I talk about Dr. Madhav Patil, a person who is very important to me. His presence is a steady reminder of how much a mentor can change a person's life and how a legacy of kindness can last for a long time. I feel a deep sense of gratitude for the important lessons I learned from a remarkable person. His presence has left a lasting mark on my life and made me who I am now.

Embracing Challenges and Forging a New Path

During this important time in my life, I found myself on a journey through a complicated landscape of obstacles and successes. It was a time that tested my strength and resolve. It pushed me to my limits and gave me chances to grow and develop as a person. As I tried to get around this complicated scenery, I ran into a lot of problems that looked impossible at first. Still, I had a strong will and kept going.

As I think about the complicated dance that is my life, I have come to a deep understanding. It's a story with threads of both battles and victories, a delicate balance where the forces of trouble and chance work together in harmony. In the pages of this story, I invite you to join me on a trip that will change you. Together, we will get to the heart of who I am and look at the knowledge that has been etched into my soul by the hard times I've been through and the decisions I've made. I set out on a journey through landscapes that have changed my life forever, led by my own beacon of self-discovery and powered by my unwavering drive.

From the moment I was born, I instinctively understood how important hardship is to the human journey. But what makes us who we are is not the problems themselves, but how we deal with them. These words have always touched me deeply as I've gone through life. Since I was young, I've faced a lot of challenges and problems that have tried my strength and helped me become the person I am today. Growing up in a middle-class family, I quickly learned how important it is to work hard and keep going. My folks taught me to be a hard worker and to never back down from a challenge. As I went through the ups and downs of life, I learned that it's not the things that happen to us that make us who we are. Throughout my life, I've faced many challenges that have tried my strength and ability to keep going. But when things didn't go my way, I made a conscious decision to have a positive attitude and stay determined. This new viewpoint helped me grow and change in ways that went beyond my most ambitious goals.

In the big picture of my life, there is one important memory that keeps coming back to me. It shows how compassion and encouragement can have a huge effect on a person's journey of self-discovery and growth. Dr. Khedkar was watching me as I worked in a busy microbiology lab. This made me more aware of my surroundings. There was a lot of stress in the air, and I didn't know what would happen next. It was when I was caught in the web of what I thought was my own mistake and feeling lost and down. But out of the chaos came a person with an unexpectedly good trait: patience and understanding. When I think about that life-changing moment, it reminds me of how much power acts of kindness and understanding have. This amazing person, whose name I will always remember, showed a level of patience that was beyond anyone's standards. In response to what they thought was my mistake, they chose not to judge or blamc me, but instead to show me kindness. His understanding, which is so rare and valuable, wrapped around me like a warm hug. It was as if they had a natural ability to see past the surface and dig deeper. This lesson has become a cornerstone in my life. It reminds me every day of the power of a helping hand when I'm feeling weak. It has taught me that even when things look the darkest, there is always a light to guide us.

Rumi's wise words have helped me feel better and taught me a lot about life. "The wound is where the light comes in," he said, and those words have left an everlasting mark on my soul. These words have stuck with me and helped me find my way through the complicated maze of life. Over the course of my life, I've come to realise that battles, no matter how hard they are, have a huge potential to bring about big changes. Over the course of my life, I've come to see every struggle as a way to improve my character and build up my inner strength. Taking on problems with courage has been one of the most important things in my life. It has helped me grow as a person and given me a strong sense of resilience. This toughness has become my compass, letting me handle the uncertain turns and twists that life throws at me with firm resolve.

My quest for information turned into my own personal lab, where I dug deep into the worlds of understanding and enlightenment. In the big picture of my life, I've always seen myself as a magician who works hard to turn problems into valuable stepping stones that help me reach the highest level of success. Choosing to see problems as possibilities has been one of the most important things in my life. Instead of seeing them as obstacles, I've always seen them as ways to move forward. From the depths of my soul came a fiery resolve that pushed me forward to overcome every hurdle that dared to stand in my way. I set out on a journey to make my dreams come true with a strong sense of purpose.

On my journey through life, I came across Nelson Mandela's deep knowledge. His words, "I learned that courage was not the absence of fear, but the triumph over it," struck me deeply and became a guiding star that lit my way. I write about how I came to deeply understand that real courage grows when we face and beat our deepest fears. When I think about my trip, I remember

Franklin D. Roosevelt's wise words: "The only thing we have to fear is fear itself." These strong words have been a constant reminder to me to let go of my fears and take advantage of all the chances that life has to give.

My journey led me to the International Post Graduate Diploma in General Insurance programme at IIRM, Hyderabad. It was a quest for information that also helped me grow as a person. I remember the turning points that made me the person I am today. During this time, I really grew in my ability to think critically, talk to others, and work as part of a team. My horizons were broadened by talking with people in the business, who also helped me a lot on my journey.

With a strong commitment to risk management, I started an amazing journey in the insurance industry, where my career took off. This shows how determined I was to take advantage of every chance and follow my interests with all my heart. I talked about a decision that had a deep impact on me and showed me the value of always going with your heart.

When I think back on my journey, I'm thankful for the times of struggle and success that have shaped the way my life has gone. In my story, I talk about how my life has been shaped by the many difficulties I've faced and overcome with an open heart and a determined spirit. Through these hard times, I've seen how hardship can change things for the better, as it's helped me grow and become wiser. My story is a tapestry of bravery, drive, and staying strong. It's a story that sums up what life is all about.

I, the author, am standing here as a live proof of the amazing journey of self-discovery and personal growth. My life has been shaped by my ability to keep going even when things are hard and by the benefits I've gotten from going beyond my comfort zone. My story is a record of a trip that was just as interesting as where it led. My whole life, I have been driven by an intense desire to learn and experience new things. This never-ending curiosity has been the key to my personal and professional growth, putting me on the path to self-discovery and happiness. I have always been very grateful for the many chances that life gives me, and I have always taken them with both hands.

Guiding Lights: Rahul and Prashant

During my life-changing time at IIRM Hyderabad, I had the chance to meet Rahul and Prashant, who are both amazing people. These important people left an indelible mark on my life. Their unique views and deep wisdom made me a better person. As I got used to the busy city, I found myself surrounded by a friendly group of people whose presence and advice had a big impact on my outlook and helped me grow as a person.

I would be wrong not to talk about Rahul, my loyal flatmate, in my book. I will always remember how practical and down-to-earth he seemed. On my trip, I was lucky enough to meet Rahul, an amazing person who became not only a mentor but also a guiding light in my life. Through his advice and knowledge, I learned how important it is to take the lead and take full responsibility for the results I want. Rahul's impact on my journey of self-discovery and personal growth will stay with me forever. Rahul's had a huge impact on my life. Through his teaching and mentoring, I've learned to be very self-disciplined and have a lot of strength. These traits have been very important in my life and have helped me achieve a lot.

On the other hand, Prashant showed me an ethereal world that I had never been to before. It was a place where faith, meditation, and being present were important. I was drawn to his calm presence because I was interested in how sensitive and spiritually deep he seemed to be. As I, Prashant, shared what we had learned about meditation and awareness, my excitement about these practises enhanced, making me want to learn more about how they can help me in deeper ways.

Under Prashant's guidance, I went on a journey that changed me, going deep into the complicated maze of my own ideas and feelings. Through this deep study, I learned how to deal with anxiety and create a deep sense of inner calmness, which is a very useful skill. With the help of my mentor, I went on a life-changing trip that changed the way I see the world forever. Through his wise advice and constant support, I found practises that helped me think about myself and make good decisions. With these new tools, I was able to deal with the complicated parts of life with more focus and purpose. On my journey to find myself, I had the good fortune to meet Prashant, a wise and enlightened person. Under his direction, I started a deep exploration of what it means to be human, going deep into the core of what it means to be alive. Through

Prashant's lessons, I began to understand how important it is to try to find balance and inner harmony even though life is often full of chaos. His words of knowledge spoke to me on a deep level and lit a fire of understanding in my soul. As I listened to him talk, I was drawn to the idea that real happiness doesn't come from the outside world, but from the depths of our own selves. Rahul and Prashant, two people who had a big impact on my personal development, will stay with me forever. They sparked a fire in me that made me want to question what I thought I knew, be open to change, and face the unknown with unwavering drive.

When I think back on my time at IIRM Hyderabad, I can't help but feel incredibly grateful to Rahul and Prashant for how much they shaped my path. During my trip, I was lucky enough to meet an amazing mentor who not only taught me a lot but also became a close friend. Their constant help and advice helped me figure out what to do when I was in a new place and didn't know what to do next. Through my interactions with wise people, I went on a trip that changed me and helped me realise how important it is to accept your flaws, live with a purpose, and keep your life full of passion.

I had a profound realisation about what real friendship and a good mentor are all about.

As I look back on my life, it's clear that the people I've met and the relationships I've built have had a big impact on who I am today. With the unwavering direction and support of extraordinary people like Rahul and Prashant, my journey has turned into a story about finding out what I'm really good at and trying to live a life with a purpose. I am still influenced by these amazing people, and both of them are a constant source of inspiration as I move through the different parts of my life. Their powerful effect has given me a deep-seated belief in the power of embracing every step of my personal journey with an open heart and a strong commitment to personal growth and progress.

Discovering My Passion

In this exciting chapter, I'll talk about how my passions have led me down a road that has shaped my life. As a child, I had a natural sense of wonder and a never-ending desire to learn. I would spend a lot of time

As soon as I started going to college, I found myself in a world of information and understanding. Education became my guide light, showing me how to grow as a person and understand things better. With each passing day, I dove deeper into the vast sea of knowledge that awaited me. The voices of teachers and classmates echoed through the halls. Their words rang in my head and sparked a fire of curiosity and ambition in me. I started to figure out what life was all about by looking into the depths of many different topics and disciplines. I learned the power of critical thinking and the beauty of intellectual research through many hours of study and thought. I jumped at the chance to broaden my intellectual views and feed my insatiable thirst for knowledge. Like an artist with a blank canvas, I splashed bright colours of curiosity all over my academic activities without fear. I can't help but think about those exciting, change-filled years. When a new chapter started, there was always a feeling of joy and wonder.

As I started college, I couldn't stop thinking about how much I wanted to learn about dairy science. I had no idea why, but I was pulled into the fascinating world of the dairy industry. It was as if a magnetic force had grabbed my imagination and forced me to look into the complex web of connections this business had to global food security and sustainability. From my deep interest in science came a burning passion for making and processing dairy products, which changed the course of my work.

I can see that dairy technology really did represent my greatest hopes. It was a way for me to make a difference in people's lives, which had always been something I cared deeply about.

As I started to work in this area, a tapestry of awe-inspiring size and complexity opened up in front of me. As the years went by, I found that I had learned a lot about a wide range of things. Because I was interested, I looked into the complicated chemistry of milk and how dairy processing plants work. In the middle of this maze-like scenery, I ran into a lot of problems that would change the way my journey turned out in the end. In this complicated world, I learned how important it is to have a wide range of skills and knowledge.

Throughout my journey, I was lucky enough to have respected teachers who helped me develop my analytical skills and broaden my view of the world. This important event has made a deep impact on me that will last for a long time.

On my journey, I had to go through some hard times. I was determined from the start to make a name for myself in my field. This motivation pushed me forward and helped me get past any problems that got in my way.

As I start my journey through the halls of academia, I find myself going back over my past and thinking about a key time of change that changed both my character and my mind. During this important time in my life, I found myself in a place where I could grow and where the amazing promise of dairy technology was made very clear. I found a deep source of happiness and joy in this world. This haven of progress and innovation became my safe place, a place I accepted with all my heart and made a part of my life.

My story is a tapestry made up of many different events, each of which was important in making me who I am today. The problems I've solved in my life have had a big impact on my life. These things have tried my strength and taught me important lessons that have helped me grow and become wiser. When I look into the future, I get excited about all the things that could happen. I'm very excited to go on a journey to follow my interests and get better at what I already know. When I think about my trip so far, I feel like I'm standing on the edge of the unknown and looking at the long road ahead of me. Like an artist standing in front of a blank painting, I have an insatiable curiosity and can't wait to see the bright colours and intricate shapes that will make up the tapestry of my life.

Following My Dreams

After I finished college, I was eager to start my professional life and put the information and skills I had learned to use. I understand that I have always wanted to make a difference for the better in the world. This made me want to find a job that would let me do just that.

I understand that following my interests has been an important part of my journey. It has helped me not only reach my goals but also find out who I really am. I think that following our interests isn't just about getting what we want; it's also about finding out what we're here to do. As I have followed my heart and aligned myself with the universe's divine plan, my life has been full of meaning and purpose.

I read a quote from Bhagavad Gita that has stuck with me for a long time. It is said that Lord Krishna said, "The meaning of life is to find your purpose." This quote has been a guide for me as I've tried to find my life's meaning and passion. I think that each of us has something special to give the world, and it's our job to find it and share it with others. This quote has always reminded me to be true to myself and never give up on my dreams. I've always thought that giving is what life is all about. Giving is what really brings us to life. I notice that a major theme has been finding out what I have to offer the world and putting it to good use. This quote speaks to me because it shows how important it is to find your reason and make a positive difference. Throughout my journey, I've tried to figure out my skills and interests and use them in ways that matter. My path hasn't always been easy, but I'm thankful for the chances I've had to learn and make a difference. As I go through life, I am committed to staying true to myself and using my skills to help the world as a whole.

In my book, I talk about the wise words of Lord Krishna from the Bhagavad Gita that reminded me to always do my job. He taught me that doing something is always better than doing nothing. As a young adult, the saying that tells us to go after our goals and dreams without giving in to fear always gave me hope. This way of thinking has been a big part of my life, pushing me to go after my dreams and get past any problems that come up. I don't think fear should ever stop us from reaching our full potential, and I've tried to live my life with this idea in mind.

In the end, my life's journey has taught me that chasing our goals isn't just about getting what we want for ourselves; it's also about finding out what we're good at and making the world a better place. Bhagavad Gita talks about the lessons of Lord Krishna, and I have tried to follow them through my life. It is important to find and use my skills to help other people. This has helped me reach my goals and take care of my tasks in life. Lord Krishna's wisdom has helped me on my trip, and I'm thankful for the lessons I've learned along the way.

I was just getting started in my career when I ran into a whole new set of problems. I understand it was hard to find a good balance between work and my personal life. My work was often hard and overwhelming, which made it hard to keep a good balance.

When I was in a tough situation, I used the knowledge and skills I had gained in college and other parts of my life. I have used my intelligence, ability to speak well, and flexibility to get through different situations and challenges in my life.

As I worked on my job, I talked to experts in my field for advice and inspiration. I'm thankful for the people who helped me along the way and never stopped supporting me and giving me advice.

Even though I had to deal with a lot of problems, I was happy with how things turned out. As I started my journey, I ended up doing work that was very important to me. It felt like I was fulfilling all of my greatest hopes and dreams.

When I think back on this time, I'm most thankful for the chances I had to learn and grow. When I think about how far I've come so far, I'm proud of the goals I've reached and excited to see where my career goes from here.

I've reached many work and personal milestones in my life that have had a big effect on my growth and development.

One of the things I'm most proud of is being given a leadership role at my company. It was a great honour to be noticed for how hard I worked and how much I cared about the organization's goals. I worked very hard to build my reputation and show that I was worth something.

As I started my new job, I couldn't help but feel excited about the chance to make an even bigger impact. I was excited to take on the task and make a big difference because I was in charge of a group of skilled and driven professionals.

I have always liked to test myself and see how far I can go by taking on new challenges and pushing my limits. Throughout my work, I've always been eager to look for ways to improve and move up in my field. This has meant going to conferences and classes and getting different credentials and certificates to help me learn and improve.

After I got my IPG Diploma in General Insurance, I felt sure of myself and ready to take on any tasks. I was ready to start working in the field that I had spent so much time and energy learning about.

When I started working, I found out that the truth was a lot worse than I had thought. Even though I was skilled and determined, it was hard for me to find a job. After putting out a lot of resumes and going to a lot of interviews, I was sad to find out that none of them led to a job offer.

As the days turned into weeks and the weeks into months, I started to feel more and more lost and sad. After my dad retired, I kept looking for a job. Even though I was skilled and knowledgeable, I had trouble getting a job.

There were times when I didn't know where I was going or how to get there. I felt hopeless and lost because I didn't know what was going on. It was hard to find my way. As things kept getting worse, it became clear that I was having a hard time dealing with the worry and stress that came with them. At times in my life, I felt like I couldn't get out of the hole I was in. I realise that there was a time when I had a lot of self-doubt and questioned my ability to find a satisfying job that would let me use my skills to their best.

During those hard times, my loved ones' words of support kept me going. Even when my road ahead seemed dark and unclear, I remembered my strengths and kept moving forward with the help of those around me. And little by little, my life began to change. I understand that putting my knowledge of general insurance to use was a turning point. Then I felt like I had a new mission and was happy with my life.

When I think back to that hard time, I can see how it helped. I've learned over the course of my life how important it is to have a strong support system and keep a positive mood when things are hard. I remember a time when I faced a problem that seemed impossible to solve. But this taught me that no matter how hard things are right now, there is always hope for a better tomorrow. I remember a time when I was confused and unsure about my future. Even though I tried, it was hard for me to find a job path that really fit me and made me feel fulfilled. I remember a time when I had to do something very hard. No matter how hard I tried, I couldn't pass the tests needed for jobs in the insurance and banking businesses. I felt like a failure after this, but I knew I had done everything I could.

My parents were the most important people in my life because they let me take a teaching course at the National School of Banking (NSB) in Pune. This experience gave me the courage to try something new and follow my dreams. I moved away from my family and friends to start a new part of my life. Even though it was scary, I knew it was the best choice I could have made.

When I first got to NSB, I was struck by how excited and driven my new friends were. Over the next few months, I gave my all to the difficult classes at NSB. My days were long and hard because they were full of lessons, homework, and practise tests. I made up my mind to do it and worked hard on all of my tasks. My NSB masters were some of the most caring and passionate teachers I've ever met. To get ready, I worked hard and tried to do everything as well as I could. I helped myself believe in my skills, but I also had faith in myself. As I went through the course, I started to feel like my life had more meaning and direction. No longer did I feel like I had no direction and didn't know what to do. I knew what I wanted to do and was ready to do whatever it took to get there.

And in the end, everything I did and how hard I worked paid off. I'm proud of how hard I worked and how dedicated I was to getting where I am now. I never gave up, even though it wasn't always easy. I worked through the problems and setbacks, keeping my eye on the goal the whole time. Now I can say with certainty that my hard work paid off. I got a job with a top player in the financial services business after passing the entrance tests for several well-known banks and insurance companies.

When I think back on my time at NSB, I can say with certainty that it changed my life. This taught me that if you have the right help and direction, you can do anything. It also taught me how important hard work, dedication, and sticking with something are.

What I learned at NSB was possibly the most important thing I could have learned: that my idea of success shouldn't just be checking things off a list. I've learned over the course of my life that the journey is what really counts. It's not just about getting to a certain place, but also about the things you learn and grow as a person along the way. This way of thinking has helped me get through many ups and downs and enjoy every moment along the way. I will always be thankful to NSB for the education I got there and the chances it gave me in my personal and business lives.

Leaving my job was undoubtedly a challenging decision, especially considering the time and effort I had invested. However, I've come to recognise that such experiences are crucial for personal growth and have played a pivotal role in helping me understand my life's direction. This realisation became evident when I parted ways with 3 financial companies.

Starting my professional journey at filled me with excitement. The positive reputation of the company fueled my anticipation, but as I immersed myself in the role, I discovered that it didn't bring the happiness I had anticipated. Reflecting on that phase of my career, I recall a time when the work environment failed to elicit satisfaction. Despite my efforts to find value in my tasks, I realised that I needed more challenges and opportunities to make a substantial impact. With a heavy heart, I decided to leave job, seeking new prospects that would foster personal growth and allow me to contribute meaningfully to the world.

In pursuit of expanding my knowledge in the insurance sector, I transitioned to life insurance company. Although I gained valuable experience, my initial expectation of finding a sense of accomplishment fell short. Despite putting in hard work and working long hours, I struggled to feel satisfied in my role.

Seeking a fresh start, I joined cooperative bank, yet a lingering feeling persisted that something crucial was missing from my life. This phase prompted me to reassess my career path and aspirations, searching for a role that would not only challenge me but also align with my deeper sense of purpose.

The journey through these professional experiences has been a significant part of my self-discovery. It has shaped my understanding of what brings fulfilment to my career and life. As I continue my quest for meaningful opportunities,

I am determined to find a path that resonates with my passions and allows me to make a positive impact on the world.

Working at Cooperative Bank was a big deal and a big part of what made me. As an officer at a bank, I was sent to work at the teller desk, which was a surprise. It was my first job ever, and working behind the counter scared me to death. As a young person with little work experience, I found the job's tasks to be too much for me to handle. On my first day, I was able to get through all of the tasks without running into any big problems. The second day was the worst day of my life. I remember a time when I was really scared. While managing the cash counter, I encountered a significant issue during the end-of-day balance tally. It became apparent that there was a shortage of Rs. 5,000 in the cash balance. Despite my earnest efforts, I couldn't trace the whereabouts of this missing amount, and a sense of worry was evident on my face. On that day, I was sad and tired, so I chose to go home. There was obviously something wrong, and both me and my parents were scared. No matter how hard they tried to hide it, I could see the worry in their eyes. That night, it was hard for me to get to sleep. All I could think about was how much money I didn't have.

After giving it a lot of thought, I decided to quit my job at cooperative bank. When I told my parents why I thought this, they were sure and agreed with me. The next day, I chose to make a change and take charge of my life. I wrote my resignation letter and gave it to my boss. I felt relieved.

Leaving cooperative bank was hard, but it was the best choice for me in the end. I understand that this choice was a turning point in my life. I had to make a hard choice at the time, but I knew it was important for my personal and career growth. When I think about my time at the Coop Bank, I'm thankful for the things I did and the lessons I learned, but I'm also excited about the new things that are coming my way. This taught me how important it is to stop and think about different choices and points of view on my own journey. As I think about my life, I understand that it's important to check in on my progress towards my goals from time to time. Henry Ford once said, "Failure is just the chance to start over, but this time smarter." At the time, I may have seen my choice to work with the Coop Bank as a failure, but now I see it as a chance to start over and make a better choice in the future.

It's okay to let go of things that aren't helping us anymore. I had to have the guts to take a deep breath, look at the situation from a different angle, and try again. I need to tell myself the truth and realise when my wants are not being met.

Work was a big part of my life, and the only way to be truly happy is to do work that you think is great. And the only way to do good work is to be passionate about it. Don't give up if you haven't found it yet. Don't give up. Like all things of the heart, you'll know when you find it."

Leaving my jobs was a hard decision, but I knew that staying put would only bring me boredom and pain. I had to make the hard choice to leave each job one by one. I did something risky without a plan B because I thought it would help me grow as a person and in my job.

In hindsight, the best thing I could have done was to quit those jobs. When the chance came up, it made me think about my career goals again. My life has always been about trying out new things and following my interests. It's given me the chance to try out new things and find satisfaction in the things that excite me the most.

In the end, I decided that it was okay to quit a job that wasn't making me happy. I've always been okay with reevaluating my work goals. I've always thought that I should follow my heart and take chances to reach my goals. I've never been afraid of going into the unknown because I know that's often what it takes to hit new heights.

During my time at NSB Pune, I was put to the test in ways that stretched my skills and taught me important lessons about how to deal with problems. Having to struggle to make ends meet and get used to new places was a big task in my life. At the hostel, I was given a small room that was only big enough for me and two other people. I lived in a block with only one toilet for everyone. It was often dirty and unpleasant, so it was always hard to use. I understand that one of my strengths has been my ability to stay calm under pressure.

The weather has always been a tough opponent. Even though it's hard, I've learned to deal with whatever Mother Nature throws at me by adapting and keeping going. During my time in Pune, I often walked to and from the teaching place. it was hard to get through the flooded streets because the water often came up in my shoes and made it impossible to wear. Rain didn't get in the way of my day. I've always been determined to reach my goals, even when I was young. I quickly realised that the only way to be successful was to work hard and stay focused.

As a student, I went to the coaching centre and spent a lot of time learning there. I felt tired and worn out all the time, and each day felt longer than the last. No matter how hard things got, I have never given up. I forced myself to keep going because I knew that all of my hard work would pay off in the end.

But in my life, I had to deal with more than just physical problems. It was hard to deal with the stress I felt in my mind. I had tried to do something many times, but each time I was disappointed and failed. Fear and dread came over me when I thought about trying it once more. During my time in school, I had to deal with many problems, one of which was the overwhelming stress that came with taking tests. I often couldn't handle the pressure, and I struggled with feelings of helplessness and fear. I was afraid, but I got over it and did it anyway. As a student, I always paid attention to school and had faith in my own skills.

When I first got to Pune, I felt like I was from another planet. As soon as I got to the city, I couldn't figure out where I was because there was so much going on. Because I was a stranger in a new place, I didn't know anyone and felt lost in all the noise and activity. I grew up in a small town, so when I moved to the big city, I felt like I was in a different world.

Initially, fitting in was a challenge for me during my younger years. I struggled to grasp the concept of being "cool" or "hip," leading to uncertainties about how to dress or talk like those around me. Recalling those times, I vividly remember the feeling of being a stranger in a bustling city, navigating a world that felt unfamiliar. Being an outsider in that environment triggered discomfort as I grappled with the fear of standing out and facing judgment from others.

This apprehension of negative judgment lingered with me for a while. However, as time passed, I came to the realisation that I needed to cease resisting what made me different and instead embrace those unique qualities. There was a pivotal moment when I consciously decided to stop comparing myself to others and shift my focus towards acknowledging my strengths and what made me special.

It dawned on me that I am a diligent worker and a dedicated student. While I may not have considered myself the most beautiful or stylish person during my younger years, I took pride in being genuine and honest in my interactions with others. Embracing these qualities allowed me to build confidence and authenticity, helping me to navigate the challenges of fitting in while staying true to myself.

I gradually became a surer of myself and a confident person. I learned English well and got used to living in a city. I understand that I've always gone my own way. At one point, I realised that I didn't have to meet other people's standards in order to be successful. This realisation was a turning point for me, and it has changed the way I deal with challenges and chances ever since. I've always been able to stay true to myself and succeed at the same time.

During my time at NSB, I spent all of my time in the library, reading and writing whenever I could. In my book, I'd like to say that I used to get up before sunrise so I could start studying early. I was so tired from studying that I had to force myself to keep going. I did it because it was my last chance.

My life was also not very good. One of the hardest things I had to deal with was sharing a small apartment room with two other people. It was hard to find privacy and personal space in the small room, and emotions were often high. During the whole time, I lived in that dorm. Even when things got hard, I didn't lose my goal. I have always stayed focused on my goals and refused to complain about any problems that came my way.

I had some of the hardest times of my life when I studied at NSB Pune. My daily schedule was pretty set. I would get up early every morning and get ready for the day. After getting dressed, I would go to class. Every day, from 7 a.m. I would spend most of my day in classes, taking only short breaks to use the facilities. I didn't have any time to rest or sleep. When I was a student, I always put my classwork first. So, whenever I had homework that I hadn't finished, I made sure to get back to it right away. Even though I had lessons in the morning, I still had to work until the evening. After lunch, I would often go back to my desk to keep working on my schoolwork. I knew that anything less than my best attempt would not be good enough. I went to class all day, listened to talks, and took a lot of notes.

When the next group of students came in the evening, I finally had some time to myself. I would leave the building after class and go for a walk outside. I would go to the newspaper stand every day to get the latest issues and keep up with what was going on in the world.

A time when I would jump at any chance to get out of my daily schedule. One of these times was when I got to take part in an action outside of the typical classroom setting. I remember how easy things gave me peace. The sound of cars driving by in the distance and the soft breeze would calm my mind and get me ready for the difficulties ahead. After dinner, I thought about what I had learned that day. I always double-checked my notes to make sure I remembered the right information. After I finished my day's work, I would read the newspaper for a while before going to bed.

Keeping to my schedule has been a lot of work, but it has been well worth it. The reason I did so well in coaching classes was that I was very good at blocking out distractions. I've learned over the course of my life how important it is to focus on one thing at a time. These lessons have helped me in many different areas of my life.

I've always believed in the power of practice. As Malcolm Gladwell once said, "Practise isn't what you do when you're good. It's what makes you good." I am committed to putting in a lot of time and effort every day to reach my goals.

The schedule taught me how important it is to be on time. I understand that time management is one of the most important things I've learned. Through my own experiences, I've learned how to make the most of every moment and how to put things in the right order. The self-control and resolve I learned when I was young have been very helpful to me throughout my life.

I also learned how important it is to get out of the classroom for a while. I quickly learned as a young student that there was more to life than just sitting in a classroom all day. I wanted action and excitement, and I knew I had to go out into the world to really understand it. So I made it a goal to get out of class as often as I could. Whether I went out, did something outside, or just took a walk around the neighbourhood, I was able to clear my mind and get back to work. Robert Frost's words have always been a guide for me in my life. "The woods are beautiful, dark, and deep, but I have promises to keep and miles to go before I sleep." This has been my motto through many challenges and problems, telling me to stay focused on my goals and never give up. I know for sure that my time at NSB Pune was one of the most difficult and rewarding times. Because I had a busy schedule, I learned how important it is to focus, use my time wisely, and take breaks to re-energize.

I finally started to see the effects after months of hard work and dedication. As I learned more about the subject, I became more sure of myself because I understood it better. I started to believe in myself and my skills.

During my formative years, I went through a time when I grew and learned a lot. I learned that being like everyone else is not the key to success. I understand that it has been a journey of finding and accepting my true self. I've learned that the best way to reach your goals is to be sure of who you are. I think that if you want to live a happy life, you have to fight for what you want.

When I got a job at the State Bank of India (SBI), my life changed in a big way. During that time in my life, I felt a lot of happiness and freedom. I had reached a turning point in my journey after years of hard work and dedication. My hard work was finally paying off, and I was ready to move on to a new part of my life.

In my first few days at SBI, I was both excited and worried. As I started my new job, I couldn't help but feel both excited and nervous. I knew that my bosses and coworkers had high hopes for me and that I had big shoes to fill. Even though I was worried, I was eager to show what I could do and make a difference in my new job.

On my first day of work, I was excited and looking forward to going to the SBI office. As soon as I walked in, I was met by a warm and welcoming atmosphere that made me feel right at home. I joined this team because the people I met were friendly and helpful, so I knew right away that I had made the right decision. From then on, I worked with a lot of energy and excitement, eager to learn and grow with my new coworkers. When I think back on that first day, I understand that it was the start of an amazing journey that would change my career and my life in ways I could never have imagined. There, I was impressed by how professional people were and how nice the work setting was. When I first joined the team, my bosses and peers accepted me with open arms. I didn't have to wait long before I felt like I belonged to the group and was treated like one.

During my first few days at the bank, I went through training and orientation classes that taught me a lot about how the bank works and what my job is. My training was tough, and the work I did was just as tough. Every day, I became more sure of myself and my skills. As I got older and learned more about myself, I started to see my own potential and the special skills I had. I honed my skills and followed my interests with unwavering determination because I worked hard and put in a lot of effort. As I kept going on my journey, I found that the most strength and motivation came from inside me, from the confidence that I could do anything I set my mind to. When my bosses and coworkers told me I was doing a good job, I felt encouraged to keep doing my best.

For me, working at SBI wasn't just a job; it was also a great way to learn. I've always known that teamwork, dedication, and effort are important. Through many different things, I was able to learn how to analyse and solve complicated problems.

During my time at SBI, I had to deal with a few problems. There have been times when I've had problems and failed. I have failed many times over the course of my life. But I've always made sure to learn something from each one. Because of this, I have grown stronger and smarter.

Looking back, I can see that joining SBI was a great choice on my part. Having a stable job not only gave me financial security but also helped me become the person I am today in a big way. My time at SBI was a turning point in my life. It shaped my ideals and beliefs, which have been my guides ever since.

Thanks to my time at SBI, I was able to learn and improve important skills and information while working in a fast-paced and difficult environment. I will always be thankful for the time I spent there because it made me who I am now.

The presence and effect of my loving family have had a huge impact on my life. They are the reason I try to live a life with meaning and purpose.

From my oldest memories, it's easy to see how much my family has meant to me and how much they have shaped my life. I was able to build a strong base for myself with their constant help and advice. When I think about the path I've been on, it's clear that different people have had a big impact on my beliefs and taught me the importance of being honest, moral, and hardworking.

Throughout the different parts of my life, my family's constant presence has been a constant source of support. Their steady support and encouragement have helped me get through some of the hardest times I've ever been through. As time went by, my ability to connect and interact with other people grew, becoming a skill that would shape the rest of my life. With each day that went by, I got better at communicating, creating a web of connections that made my relationships with the people around me stronger. With this new skill, I was able to understand, embrace, and celebrate the unique traits that make each person a work of art in their own right. I found the comfort and motivation I needed to beat challenges and move closer to achieving my goals in the loving embrace of this caring and supportive community.

My family's effects were felt far beyond the walls of the home we shared. My unwavering belief in myself was a pushing force that made me want to work hard and do well in everything I tried. I was motivated by how happy I was with what I had done, which helped me face problems head-on and seize chances with unwavering determination.

Finishing my education is a big step in my life that brings me and the people I love a lot of joy and happiness. In the story of my life, I talk about a time when we were all very happy and felt like we were all in it together. The moment I saw the bright smiles on my parents' faces while holding tight to the degree I had worked so hard to get will always stay in my mind. The monument sits tall as a sign of how much my parents always helped me and how hard I worked to do well in life.

Making my family and friends proud meant more than just doing well in school. It touched every part of my life and made me who I am at my very core. As I started my career, I carried the hopes and dreams of others with me. This made me even more determined to go beyond my own limits and hit heights that were even higher than I had imagined. Every improvement and success in my life became a shared victory that showed how close we were.

Not only did my work help me reach my goal of making my family and friends happy, but so did other things. As I've gone through life, I've learned to have a deep sense of compassion, awareness, and understanding. The values that my family taught me helped me become a rock of support for a close friend who was struggling with sadness and anxiety. This event was a turning point in my life because it showed me how important it is to be there for others and listen to them. I was on a personal journey of self-discovery and growth, and this event was a powerful reminder of that. It showed the deep truth that gaining the respect and pride of the people closest to us is more important than achieving great things. Rather, it depends on living by good values that lift up and inspire.

When I think about this part of my life, I feel a deep sense of gratitude, because it's during this time that I've come to truly value the strong ties that have played a key role in keeping my spirit strong along the way. My family gave me a deep sense of pride and purpose from the very beginning of my life. Their steady advice and support turned into a map that helped me navigate the rough seas of life, guiding me through both struggles and successes. Throughout my life, I've been lucky to be surrounded by people who have always shown me love and support. Their presence has had a big effect on my personal growth, affecting the decisions I've made and the paths I've taken.

Over the course of my life, a powerful story has come together, one that honours not only my own growth but also the growth of the community as a whole. In the story of my life, which is like a tapestry, the deep lines of family pride and purpose tell a story. The fact that I was given a legacy of dignity and importance keeps me going in my quest to live an important and influential life.

Connectedness and Community

As I look at the intricate tapestry of my life, I am struck by the profound fact that my relationships have been the most vibrant and life-changing threads. Over the course of my life, I've had the chance to make a lot of relationships that have helped me become the person I am today. These connections, which range from long-lasting friendships to deep ties I've made through being involved in my community, have been the basis of my personal growth and change.

During the years when I was growing up, I was lucky enough to meet a small group of people who became the pillars of my life's journey. Their understanding and support helped me find my way through life's challenges. On my trip through life, I met a lot of different people, but there was one soul in particular that touched me deeply. Together, we set out to find all the amazing things that life had to offer, turning every moment into an adventure.

As my life went on, I came to deeply understand how important it was to accept differences in my social circle. In my book, I talk about the turning points in my life when seeking out different points of view and ways of living became an important part of my journey. Participating in community projects has been a key part of my life, helping me to learn more and make a big difference. On my trip, I had the chance to meet a lot of interesting people, each of whom had a rich tapestry of stories and experiences to tell.

The fire that started in me to bring about good change became my driving force and led me to do things that mattered. I've always been pulled into projects that bring people together for a common goal. I don't know why. Whether it was the exciting job of building playgrounds or the passionate advocacy for different social causes, I was always deeply involved in projects that brought people together and encouraged them to work together. Through my work with others, I was able to make friendships that will last a lifetime and see how the power of working together can change lives.

These experiences have left a lasting mark on me and changed the way I look at the world. I've learned something very important: real relationships are very powerful. These relationships have an amazing ability to go beyond borders, creating deep empathy and understanding that makes it easy to cross gaps. In my book, I think about how shared goals can change the world and help fix the broken parts of society. Throughout my life, I've seen firsthand the amazing power that can come from a group of people working together towards a shared goal. From my formative years, I was fascinated by the idea that we could tell a story that included everyone and showed kindness, one that went beyond the differences that often separate us. This idea became a big part of my journey, influencing what I did and how I made decisions. As I learned to deal with the many challenges of life, I saw many times how powerful it was to have the same goals. Whether it was working on community projects with like-minded people or having deep conversations with people from different backgrounds, I saw the amazing things that can be done when people work together towards a shared goal.

When I think about the amazing journey of my life, I feel an overpowering sense of thanks. It's the deep ties and relationships I've made with other people that have made my life so much better. Every person I've met in my life, whether for a short time or for a long time, has had a big impact on the complex fabric of my personal journey. These links have given me a deep sense of richness and vitality that runs through my whole being. I've had a lot of experiences in my life that have taught me something important. These events have been a steady reminder that we have the incredible power to get rid of bias and intolerance when we work together with unity and empathy. Instead, we can make a beautiful story about togetherness and having the same goals.

As I move forward, my unwavering commitment to building real relationships and making good changes has become the most important thing in my life. Throughout my life, I've had the chance to get to know a lot of people from different backgrounds. Not only have these exchanges made my life more interesting, but they have also taught me important lessons that continue to shape my path. The knowledge I've gained from these links has become a guiding light, illuminating my path and encouraging me to keep working towards understanding and unity. Each experience has taught me how important it is to have compassion, understanding, and an open mind. I have learned that we can build a more peaceful world if we accept our differences and look for things we have in common. It has not always been easy to learn these things. There have been times when we didn't understand each other or agreed on something, but I've learned that these are chances for growth. By having open and respectful conversations, I've been able to break down boundaries and get closer to other people. Bringing people together and helping them understand each other is why I've been through a lot of complicated situations in my life, which has given me a deep understanding that fixing the fabric of our world is a job we all have to do. I have taken on the duty that each of us shares by putting together the threads of connection, compassion, and a shared sense of purpose.

In this book, the most important part of my trip is not my own thoughts, but the complex web of important connections. I have spent my whole life making a beauty, like a skilled weaver. Over the years, I've made connections with important people who have had a big impact on how I've grown as a person. These links have woven themselves into the fabric of my life in a way that shows the deep beauty that comes from people's lives coming together.

Resilience Under Rainstorms: Navigating Life's Trials and Triumphs

Since the beginning of my life, I have faced many challenges that have tried the depths of my mental and spiritual strength and resilience. But determination has always been one of the most important things in my life. It pushes me to overcome any problems that come up and come out even better than before. Even though I was going through a lot of hard times, I set out on a trip that helped me become the person I am today. Along this hard path, I learned some of life's most important lessons and found a source of inner power I didn't know I had.

As I've grown as a person, I've come to deeply understand how important it is to be able to get back up when things go wrong. When I think about my life, I am aware of the deep truth that the journey to self-realisation is a journey that people from all walks of life can relate to. I've always wanted to reach my full ability. Like many other people, I've had to deal with a lot of problems and obstacles on my trip. But I have never let any of these failures stop me from going after my dreams and goals. Instead, I have looked at them as chances to learn and grow as a person.

With each problem I've solved, I've learned something new and got the strength I need to deal with life's twists and turns. Through these things, I've learned the true power of resolve and what it means to be able to rise above any problem. As I continue on my path to self-discovery and fulfilment, I am sure that I will continue to face challenges head-on. Through my own journey of persistence and unwavering determination, I have come to understand the incredible power we have to make our dreams come true. My life has been anything but easy. On this trip, I've run into a lot of problems that, at times, seemed impossible to solve. During these times, I've found it important to draw on my own willpower and toughness. I have come to realise that the true essence and effect of my ideas can only be understood when put next to the beauty of nature and shown through concrete examples.

I've always been fascinated by the bamboo tree's unbreakable spirit and strength. Throughout my trip, natural metaphors have helped me feel better and given me ideas. They have been a guiding force and a steady reminder of how important it is to be determined and strong. As I think about my life, I'm aware of how the bamboo tree can be seen as a powerful metaphor. Throughout my life, I've been fascinated by the bamboo tree's unique traits. It has always amazed me how strong it is in the face of hard times. Even though I have a soft personality, I have learned to be incredibly flexible and adaptable to the challenges that life throws at me while staying strong and unbreakable.

During my time in Pune, I had a one-of-a-kind chance to start a journey of personal and career growth. During this time, I spent a lot of time in intense preparation sessions, working hard to improve my skills and knowledge for the tough banking test. I spent a lot of time in the busy city of Pune working hard to reach my school goals. As I worked hard on my training courses every day, I felt like I was getting somewhere. I didn't know it at the time, but this one event would change the rest of my life in ways I never could have imagined.

When I was standing in the middle of a torrential downpour and was soaked to the bone, I felt very tired and powerless. I was standing there when I realised that everything I was wearing, from my shoes to my socks, was totally soaked. As my eyes filled with tears, I couldn't help but feel a lot of different feelings.

As I stood there with raindrops hitting my face, memories rushed into my head and took me back to the many times I had been in similar situations. As I waited for the bus at the bus stop in the pouring rain, I felt powerless and vulnerable. Over the years, I had grown used to a certain feeling too much. But even though it was hard and annoying, I knew that this was only a small part of my trip. I understand there have been many times when I've had to face problems head-on. These problems have made me stronger and more determined, and have helped me become the person I am today. My life has been like a roller coaster, with both high points and low points that have helped me become the person I am today. I stood there, drenched to the bone, and thought about the path that had led me to this point. As I thought about all the things that had changed my life, I felt a deep sense of pride and thankfulness. I had to make a choice as I stood there in the middle of a sudden rainstorm. Should I be patient and wait for the rain to stop, or should I keep going even though I don't know how long this downpour will last? In my book, I talk about the moment when I made up my mind to face any problem that came my way, no matter what Mother Nature did.

As I stood in the cold rain, determination filled my heart. In the course of my life, I came to deeply understand that I couldn't control the forces of the world. The bus timetable, which was set by a separate entity, and the weather, which was up to the whims of nature, were things I couldn't change. But amid these things I couldn't change, I found a remarkable power within myself: the ability to control how I respond. When I felt like there was no way out, I had to decide whether to give up and give in to the overwhelming feeling of hopelessness or to keep going with unwavering drive. I decided to keep going, even though it seemed like the odds were against me because I was determined.

At that very moment, I learned a very important truth that would guide me in everything I did in the future. I have learned throughout my life that it is very wise to embrace and make the most of the potential in every situation, no matter how good or bad it seems. As a successful person, I have always put saving money for the future at the top of my list of priorities. I've always been very sure that it's important to put time and money into yourself. This idea has helped me grow and move forward all the time. So, as the careful creator of my own fate, I carefully conduct the music of my life, making sure that each note is carefully written and in tune. I carefully plan the path for tomorrow, sewing together the threads of my past successes into a tapestry of my hopes and dreams. These victories, which are like strong walls, are the foundation on which I will build the great things I will do in the future. Since the beginning of my life, I have had to face many trials and problems that have tried my strength and ability to keep going. I have always held on to the unshakeable idea that better days are just around the corner. Throughout my life, I've had to deal with a lot of problems that have tried to determine how strong I am. But when things were hard, I always reminded myself of a basic truth that has helped me: I have the strength to keep going. This powerful realisation has been a steady source of motivation for me, helping me get past problems and succeed. My unwavering positivity has helped me get through hard times and reach my goals.

I've found that keeping a cheerful attitude has helped me become stronger and more determined. I've learned that it's easy to give in to depression and hopelessness when things are hard. I've learned throughout my life that training yourself to look for the good in things can help you find happiness even in the worst situations.

For me, it has been an important part of my life to put happiness and satisfaction first, even when things are hard. Throughout my life, I've learned that having strong, good relationships with other people has helped me stay grounded and motivated during hard times. Whether it was spending time with loved ones, following my hobbies, or thinking about my own thoughts and feelings, these interactions with other people have always given me strength and inspiration.

Despite my fears and doubts, one of the most important things in my life has been to take risks and follow my hobbies. The only way to get past problems is to keep going through them, no matter how hard they are.

toughness and fortitude aren't just buzzwords; they're important tools that have helped me get through any problem. I've learned that when things are hard, I can get through them by depending on my inner strength and sticking with it. I have been able to get through hard times and come out stronger on the other side by having a growth attitude, taking calculated risks, and asking for help from my community.

Even though I studied hard, I often felt nervous on the day of a test, even though I had done everything I could to get ready. I understand that anxiety and pressure have always been with me whenever something important is at stake. I always felt the weight of demands on my shoulders, whether it was a job interview, a big presentation, or a very important test. I always wanted to do my best, so I worked harder and pushed myself further. These events taught me how important it is to be ready, to keep going, and to be strong when bad things happen. Nothing strange happened on the day of my SBI PO test. Even though I had done everything I could to be ready, the weight of expectations and responsibilities was heavy on my shoulders.

When I woke up the morning of the test, I felt a lot of different things. Months were spent getting ready for this. There were a lot of hours spent learning and taking practise tests. I couldn't help but feel the weight of duty on my shoulders as I did my best. I always felt like people had high hopes for me. Not only did I want to reach my own goals, but I also wanted to make my family happy. They had done so much to give me the tools I needed to achieve, and I didn't want to let them down. Even though the pressure was high, it made me work harder and try to do my best in everything I did.

As I walked to the testing centre, my mind was full of thoughts. Even though I tried to stay calm, I couldn't help but feel anxious. Everyone around me seemed to have high hopes for my future, and I couldn't get rid of the feeling that I had to live up to those hopes. As I looked ahead, I was motivated to do my best, but I had a nagging fear that I might not be able to reach my goals.

As I walked into the testing centre, I took a deep breath and told myself to stay calm and pay attention to the job at hand. As I walked through the halls, I couldn't help but think back to my own days as a student. Students were rushing to get to the rooms where they were supposed to take their tests. As soon as I walked into the room, I felt a familiar feeling of dread. I had felt like that many times before, but it never seemed to get better. Everyone could feel the anxiety, and they all seemed to be on edge. Even though I was nervous about what was coming, I knew I had to push through and face whatever was coming. As I sat down at my desk and opened the test book, I felt a wave of worry wash over me.

During my time in school, I had to answer difficult test questions in a short amount of time. Even though I was scared, I didn't give up. As I tried to keep my mind on the job at hand, I couldn't help but think about the many hours of work and planning that had led up to this point in my life. I tried to get rid of the weight of what other people thought of me, but it didn't work.

As I took the test, my thoughts kept going back to my responsibilities and what other people were looking forward to. I remember a time when the fear of failing was all I could think about. The thought of letting down not only myself but also the people I cared about most also made me feel bad. At times, the demands that had been put on me were too much for me to handle.

I didn't give in to the negative thoughts I had. I told myself that I was ready because I had done everything I could. I always tried to be ready for anything, and this was a repeating theme in my life. It started when I was young and learned how important it was to be bold and take charge of my own life. As I got older, this way of thinking helped me in both my personal and business life. It gave me the confidence and ease to take on challenges. When I look back, I'm proud of who I've become and the ideals that have helped me get here. I tried not to let the bigger picture overwhelm me, so I focused on the here and now, answering each question as it came up in my life story.

As the end of the test got closer, I felt a lot of different things. Even though I was glad it was over, I couldn't help but feel worried about what would happen next. I couldn't stop thinking about whether or not I had done enough to meet the high goals I had set for myself.

I had to take a hard test, but I was confident that I could do well. I tried not to get upset and answered each question calmly. After I finished the test, I felt relieved and proud of myself. When I had done everything I could, I knew there was nothing else I could do.

In the weeks that followed, I couldn't help but wait and wonder what would happen next. I was careful because I knew there was a lot of competition and I didn't have any guarantees. I was sure I did my best on the test and didn't leave anything to chance.

When the results were finally shown, my eyes filled with tears. I got to the next stages of the selection process, which were the interview and panel talk. Having done this, I felt very happy and like I had done well.

When I found out I had passed the written test for the SBI PO selection process, that was the most important moment of my life. I will always remember that day. It was a turning point on my way to becoming successful in my work. Before the written test, I had studied and worked hard for hours and hours. I remember when I was looking for a job. I knew there would be a lot of competition, so I made sure to get ready well. I know that I have always been very sure of myself. I was sure that if I worked hard and didn't give up, I could do anything I set my mind to. This unshakeable faith gave me the drive to go after my goals and try to be successful.

When I think back on that day, I realise that it wasn't just the success that made it important to me. When I think about my life, I can't help but think about how I got to where I am now. I spent a lot of time learning and getting ready for tests, and I can still remember the worry and doubt I had to get over. But I was able to get over my fears and reach my goals because I worked hard and didn't give up. My strong sense of purpose and constant drive helped me get where I wanted to be in my career. Even when I ran into problems, I stayed determined and focused on my goals.

I learned important things by taking the SBI PO written test that will help me for the rest of my life. As a child, I learned how important it is to plan ahead, keep going, and work hard. As I've gone through life, I've learned that the road to success is just as important as the goal itself. This taught me that if you work hard and don't give up, you can solve any problem, no matter how big it seems.

The most important day of my life was when I found out I had passed the written test for the SBI

PO selection process. It turned out to be a big turning point in my career, and I learned a lot about how important it is to work hard and stay focused on your goals. That day will always stand out in my mind as a day when I did something great.

There have been times in my life when I felt the weight of duty and expectation. I've felt trapped many times by the pressure to do well and the fear of failing. Whether it was studying for a test, going on a job interview, or trying to reach a personal goal, the weight of the demands could be too much. I've always tried to do my best in everything I've done in my life. I'm sure that putting in my best effort is all I can do, and that's always enough. This way of thinking has helped me be successful in many areas of my life, and I continue to follow it every day.

The day I attended the SBI PO selection process interview in Mumbai remains etched in my memory as a pivotal moment in my life. Advancing in my career was always a significant goal for me, and I was determined to seize the opportunity when it presented itself.

Walking into the venue with my father by my side instilled a sense of confidence. After investing considerable time and effort in preparation, I felt well-prepared to confront any challenges that awaited me.

My first task involved leading a group discussion on a topic I was knowledgeable about. As I gained confidence in my abilities, expressing my thoughts and opinions became more natural. Whether addressing a small or large audience, I discovered that I could articulate my ideas clearly and confidently. This skill soon became integral to both my personal and professional lives, facilitating meaningful connections with others and enabling effective communication. My openness to considering different perspectives has fostered positive collaborations, allowing us to devise logical plans and make compelling cases. Witnessing the power of teamwork and synergy during this process was immensely satisfying.

The group discussion lasted about 20 minutes, and it concluded successfully. As I stepped into the interview room, a mix of nerves and excitement accompanied me. I understood the importance of delivering my best performance, particularly in front of seasoned experts with a wealth of experience.

As I thought back on my life, I understood that I had learned about and worked in many different fields. From the time I studied dairy science to the time I worked in insurance, I had learned about a lot of different things. One thing that stands out in my mind is when I was surprised by how many questions I was getting. Even though the questions were very different, I was able to answer them by drawing on my various experiences. I kept my cool and answered each question as best I could, using what I knew and had done before.

At the end of the conversation, I felt a wave of happiness wash over me. I always gave everything I did my all, so I knew I had always done my best. I couldn't help but feel proud and accomplished as I left the interview room. It was a big step towards my job goals.

When I think about it now, that day was a turning point in my life. I remember a time when my knowledge, skills, and determination were all put to the test.

I am surprised by how strong and flexible I have become. As a person, I've learned that it's important for my growth and progress to be able to adjust to my surroundings. Life has given me a lot of problems, but I've always found a way to solve them and get ahead. I have learned to adapt to my surroundings and make the most of what I have, just like a plant. As a person, I've learned how important it is to be able to deal with problems and come back from them. I've learned that it's important to be flexible and open-minded in order to deal with life's problems.

The day of my SBI PO interview was a turning point in my quest to be happy in my job. Throughout my life, I've learned how important it is to be persistent and flexible, as well as how important it is to build good relationships with other people. I became more confident in my skills and learned the importance of working with others and as part of a team through my experiences. I will always remember the trip I had and the lessons I learned from it.

The end result was the day I had been looking forward to for a long time. The things that happened that day would change the course of my life in a big way. I've always worked hard, and I've never been afraid of a task. When I wanted to do something, I did it to the best of my ability. For me, there was no middle ground; I was all in. So when I had to do something really hard, I knew I had to give it everything I had. I couldn't go back on my word or give up. I had to do my best and give it everything I had. And I did just that. On that day, I felt nervousness, worry, and joy, among other things.

As I sat down to look at my number, my hands started to sweat and my heart started to beat faster. I thought the wait would last forever. I knew I had worked hard and done my best, but I couldn't get rid of the thought that something wasn't quite right. When I think about what I've done so far in my life, I can't help but wonder if it's been enough. Have I done everything I set out to do? Have I made the world around me a better place? As I go on my trip, these are the questions that keep me up at night. I can't help but wonder what would have happened if I hadn't learned anything important in my life. It's scary to think about, but I've had to deal with it. Every mistake I've made and every success I've had has taught me something important about myself and the world around me. I may not have all the answers, but I'm glad I've learned some things along the way.

As the highly anticipated day arrived, the culmination of my efforts and sacrifices, I awaited the verdict that would determine whether I had secured a coveted position. A particular moment from that day stands out vividly in my memory—an overwhelming mix of happiness and relief that left me momentarily speechless. Having overcome numerous challenges and sacrifices, I could finally declare with pride that I had achieved my dream of becoming a probationary officer at SBI.

My immediate impulse was to share the news with my rock, my father, who had been a constant pillar of support throughout the journey. His joy and pride in my accomplishment were palpable through the phone, reinforcing the significance of having someone steadfast in my corner, and providing guidance and encouragement when needed.

Informing my sisters and those dear to me unleashed a wave of genuine happiness and congratulations. The ensuing moments of celebration and shared joy underscored the importance of having a supportive network of people who genuinely cared about my achievements.

In the aftermath of that transformative day, the realisation dawned upon me that it held the power to shape the trajectory of my life. This singular event marked the beginning of a new chapter, providing not only a sense of accomplishment but also the motivation and direction necessary for the journey ahead. Reaching this lifelong goal became the catalyst for my newfound drive and purpose, setting the stage for the next phase of my life.

The road ahead was not going to be easy, and I knew that. As a probationary officer in the SBI, I had to do several tasks and pass several tests. I was getting ready for it. I set out on a journey to reach my goals, full of excitement, determination, and drive. I've spent my whole life trying to get better, learn new things, and make a good difference in the world around me.

When I look back on my life, I can see that it was about more than just me. Throughout my life, I've been lucky to have the help of many people who have helped me along the way. I owe a debt of gratitude to all of them, from my beloved family members to my best friends to my respected teachers. I wrote a special part of my book just for them to show how much they meant to me. As a person who works well with others, I always do my best to help the group do well. Even though I may have only had a small part in what we did, I am glad to have been a part of what the team did.

On that day, I learned how important it is to be dedicated, persistent, and sure of myself. I understand that one of the most important things I've learned is that the path to success is just as important as the success itself. As a child, I learned how important it is to be thankful and to never take anything for granted. This lesson has stuck with me my whole life, and I'm still grateful for everything I have.

As my career went on, I became more and more aware that new obstacles and chances would come up. I was ready to face problems with the same determination and hope that had helped me get where I am now.

When I got the final result, my life changed in a big way. It was a day that changed the way my life would go from then on. I understand that there was a time when I didn't know where I was going or why I was here. But I found comfort in something that showed me where to go and what to do. I learned how important it is to work hard, keep going, and have faith in one's own skills. This day will always be important to me, and I will think about it with great joy.

Chasing Dreams, Embracing Victories: A Symphony of Achievements

Since I can remember, I have always been able to find happiness in even the smallest victories and celebrate the most important ones. Through all the stages of my life, I've always found reasons to celebrate. My life's tapestry is made up of many threads of success. Each one represents a big step forward, a useful lesson learned, or a long-held goal that I've reached. These times, like a mirror, show me how far I can go and show how determined I have always been.

In the grand theatre of my life, I've taken the middle stage with grace and basked in the glory of my amazing accomplishments. Every time I took a step towards my dreams, I found myself gladly opening my arms to the applause of self-recognition. I've always enjoyed enjoying my successes, no matter how big or small they were. I have made it a point to honour the hard work that went into each success, whether it's with a simple nod of happiness or a big party with family and friends.

As I bask in the bright light of the stage, my thoughts go beyond my own achievements. Throughout my life, I have grown to deeply value the knowledge I have gained. I have grown and changed as a person because of the different obstacles I have faced. Even though these problems have been hard at times, they have helped me grow as a person and learn more about myself. I will always be grateful to the amazing people who have stood by my side throughout this amazing journey and never stopped supporting and encouraging me. Their presence has always given me strength and motivation, helping me move forward even when things were hard. When I think about the road I've been on, I'm grateful for the lessons I've learned, the strength I've gained, and the relationships I've built. Each event has made me the person I am today. During my journey, I've learned that every milestone I've reached wasn't just because of my own hard work. Instead, it was because of the amazing power of teamwork and the shared goals of those around me.

During the course of my life, I've been on an amazing trip that's been carefully paved with steps that have meaning. I have never given up on my dreams and have worked hard to get closer and closer to where I want to be. From my humble beginnings in the sacred halls of education, I set out on a trip that would change the course of my life. With a strong drive to achieve and a strong desire to learn, I took on the challenges of the business world with unwavering resolve. I will never forget the important things I learned in school. I made hard work my driving principle, and it helped me move forward even when things were hard. I learned that the way to open doors of chance was to work hard and keep going. Integrity has also become an important part of who I am. I knew how important it was to be honest and open with people, because I knew that trust was the basis for long-lasting relationships. I tried to be a person of integrity in my personal and professional life so that people would accept and admire me. But maybe the most important thing about me was that I was always hungry for growth. I realised that true success wasn't just about getting things, but also about learning new things and getting better at what I already knew. I took advantage of every chance to learn and grow. Throughout my life, I have used these beliefs as my compass, which has led me to strive for excellence.

My story shows that trying to be great is not something you do by yourself. Instead, it is a symphony of hard work and perseverance. On my way to success, I've been lucky to have amazing mentors, helpful friends, and great coworkers. Their company and advice have been very important in helping me reach higher heights. Throughout my journey, I've been lucky to have people who have always been there for me and given me advice. Their support has made me more determined and helped me hit new heights. Their help has given me the tools and information I need to deal with the problems that have come my way. And their friendship has given me a sense of connection and unity, which has helped me to do well. I will always be grateful to them for how important they were to my success.

The day I got that acceptance letter from SBI was a turning point in my life. It was the result of many years of hard work and a sign of how far I had come. It shows how hard I worked, how many hours I spent learning, how many sleepless nights I spent getting ready, and how much I believed in myself. As I started this new part of my life, I was determined to make the most of every chance that came my way.

During my teens, I was filled with an unquenchable desire to succeed, which pushed me forward on a road with many options. I found comfort and direction in the loving embrace of my parents, who taught me a set of ideals that would shape the person I would become. People around me taught me that the key to success is a combination of hard work, honesty, and commitment that never changes. As I went through school, I found that I was led by a set of rules that would eventually shape my career in banking. During this time, I worked hard to improve my skills and build a solid foundation on which I could build my business.

As soon as I started going to college, I was looking for ways to use what I had learned outside of the classroom. During my journey, I was involved in a lot of internships and other events outside of school. These events were my training ground and helped me become the person I am today. They taught me a lot about the business I was interested in and gave me practical tips that I still use today. These events helped me become more determined to be successful in the world of business.

On my way to SBI, I had to go through a lot of tough tests, interviews, and reviews. Still, being the strong person that I am, I took on every task with open arms, seeing them as golden chances to show how strong and determined I really am. I immersed myself in teaching courses, asked for advice from professionals with years of experience, and spent countless hours improving my skills. I did this because I had an insatiable desire to learn and a strong drive to succeed.

When I joined SBI, it wasn't just a step up in my job; it was also a step into a world of possibilities that would change the way my life turned out. I was excited about the steep learning curve ahead of me and ready to take on the challenges that were coming. During my journey of professional and personal growth, I had the chance to work with great colleagues and learn about many different areas. These events helped me learn new things and get better at what I already knew.

As I've moved through the world of banking, I've learned that obstacles are an important part of my path. I notice that I have always looked at every challenge as a chance to grow and improve myself. Throughout my career, I've had the chance to work in different areas and locations. These events have helped me become thc flexible and adaptable person I am today. By working in different places and taking on different tasks, I have been able to develop a set of skills that is well-rounded and covers a wide range of areas. Throughout my trip, I worked hard to improve my leadership skills and was always looking for ways to learn and grow. With each new job, I took on the tasks that came my way and managed teams with unwavering determination and a strong desire to succeed. My constant drive to do my best became a driving force that helped me move forward on my road to personal and professional growth.

Even though it was hard, I, stuck to my ideals of honesty, fairness, and skill. Values were not just words that shaped my career; they were the solid basis on which I built my professional journey. By sticking to these values throughout my job, I've earned the respect and trust of both my coworkers and my clients. This has made it clear that I am a trustworthy and honest worker.

My time with SBI has been nothing but a life-changing experience that has left an indelible mark on both my work and my personality. I have worked my way up through the ranks of the banking industry and am now a highly recognised professional. Every success I've had has added a new part to the interesting story of how I've grown as a person. When I think about my trip so far, I'm excited and looking forward to the road that lies ahead, which is full of endless potential and promise.

As I sit here with a pen in my hand writing this part of my story, I think about how important it is to recognise and remember one's accomplishments. I've learned over the course of my life that every success, no matter how big or small, is a great example of the strength of never giving up. As I raise a glass to toast my accomplishments, I am reminded that each of us has limitless potential. I've learned to respect the amazing journey I'm on because I've had to face challenges, reach new heights, and leave an indelible mark on the fabric of life.

Reflections on Life Experiences

A Start from Nothing, I took my first breath in the small town. This was the start of an amazing trip filled with strength and divine guidance. I came from a small family, so my parents taught me early on the value of hard work and determination.

When I think about how my life has come together, I feel a deep sense of awe and thankfulness. The amazing journey I've been on to get to this point is nothing short of amazing. From the first twist and turn that started my journey to the countless successes and failures that have shaped my path, my life has become a unique tapestry of experiences. In this part of my story, I'm deep in thought, thinking about the lessons that life has taught me and how important they are. Through the hard times I've been through, I've become stronger and tougher than I ever was before. During these times of self-reflection, I have found a guiding light that lights up my path and leads me towards a better future.

From the start of my trip, I've had the chance to see the wide range of things that life has to offer. From the thrilling peaks that filled me with indescribable joy to the difficult valleys that tested my resolve to the limit, my journey has given me a deep understanding of the valuable lessons that come with living a life to the fullest. Throughout my life, I've had a lot of different situations that have had a big impact on who I am today. These experiences have not only left a lasting mark on my personality but have also given me an unshakeable belief in the power of persistence and the strength that is in each and every one of us.

On my way through life, I've faced a lot of problems that have tested my strength. But it's because of these hard times that I've learned how the power of the mind and the skills of the body are so closely linked. Through my own journey, I've learned how important it is to make sure my thoughts and deeds are in sync. This important lesson has given me the strength to overcome every problem that has come my way. Through the difficulties I've faced on my journey, I've learned that the key to being strong is to combine the strength of the mind with the strength of the body. These things have made me the kind of person who faces problems with unshakable determination and a stronger sense of toughness.

When I think about the complex web of relationships that have made up my life, I am struck by how important it is to have a network of people who care about and support you. I've been lucky to have a strong network of family, friends, and coworkers to help me through my life. These amazing people have been very important to me on my journey. They have always been there for me when I had doubts and given me ideas when I didn't know what to do. Their presence has played a big role in making me who I am now. My unfailing faith and support have always been what pushes me forward and makes me want to reach for the stars.

My comfort zone has changed a lot over time. It has grown and given me access to a world full of endless options. This slow change has given me the freedom to leave my comfort zone and start a journey of self-discovery and growth. Trying new things has been a defining part of my life because it has helped me find hidden skills and parts of myself I hadn't known about before. Getting past the limits I put on myself has been one of the most important parts of my trip, showing me how much-untapped potential I have. This experience has made me want to accept the unknown with all my heart and welcome it with open arms.

When I think about the different parts of my life, I remember the goals I've reached and the dreams I've come true. But I know very well that my story is far from over. The fabric I've made throughout my life is a powerful sign of how much I've changed. Each thread was carefully picked up and woven in a way that shows how my many victories, struggles, and discoveries about myself have made me who I am today. But when I look at this beautiful tapestry, I remember that my trip is far from over. I want to keep exploring, learning, and growing because there is a whole world of events just waiting to be found. When I think about my journey so far, I feel a deep sense of thankfulness that fills my whole heart. I'm standing on the edge of the future, ready to start the next part of my life, and I'm very excited about it. The mysteries that lie ahead of me call to me, and I can't wait to figure them out because I know they will lead to new adventures and deep growth.

In the grand symphony of my life, I have danced beautifully to the beautiful tunes of happiness and bravely weathered the storms of sadness. The journey I've started is a reflection of my own unique path and a sign of the unwavering drive that runs through me. Using the brushes of courage, resilience, and unwavering purpose, I have carefully painted a masterpiece over the course of my life.

On my journey through life, I've been lucky enough to come across Lord Krishna's wise lessons. I've learned the delicate balance between detachment and devotion because of his divine knowledge. On my journey, I've been lucky enough to learn from an amazing person. These lessons have been a constant source of inspiration for me and have given me the tools I need to deal with life's challenges with grace and humility. During my journey of self-discovery, I've been lucky enough to learn deep lessons about not being attached and being dedicated. These important lessons have changed the way I see the world and given me a new sense of purpose and knowledge. I think one of the most important things I've learned is to do my best without getting attached to the results. This way of thinking has freed me from the chains of demands and let me fully enjoy the moment I'm in. I have found a deep sense of freedom and inner peace by letting go of my attachment to certain results. In my quest for personal and professional growth, I've come to realise that everything I do is a step on the way to getting better at myself. Every event, whether it was a success or a failure, has given me a chance to learn and grow. This realisation has given me the strength to face every task with courage and hope, knowing that there is always room for growth, even when things are hard. I have learned to accept the uncertainty that comes with life through the lessons of nonattachment and dedication. Instead of letting fear or worry control what I do, I have built up a deep trust in the way life works. This trust has helped me handle the twists and turns of my journey with grace and resilience, knowing that every event is a lesson in disguise. As I continue on this road of self-discovery, I am grateful for the deep lessons that Lord Krishna has taught me. They have made me a source of strength and knowledge. During my travels, I've had the good fortune to meet a wise person whose words have left an everlasting mark on my soul. The important things I've learned from him have shown me what moral strength really means and how important it is to live a life that is completely in line with one's values. I have found the deep courage I have inside me through my unwavering commitment and desire to give up. Because of my courage, I've been able to get through life's storms and come out on the other side stronger than before.

The sound of the Hare Krishna chant has been with me at every step of my life's journey. Since I was a child, when I was still innocent and full of wonder, my motto has been a source of comfort and peace. It has always reminded me of my eternal connection to a greater power and helped me figure out how to deal with the complicated parts of being an adult. "Hare Rama, Hare Rama, Rama Rama, Hare Hare" has been a part of me for my whole life. Its sounds have been woven into the very fabric of my being. These holy sounds have been a steady anchor in times of trouble and a source of comfort in the chaos that is often all around us. In addition, they have been like a compass, leading me to a place of deep inner peace and unity.

The path I've taken through life has been an amazing journey of finding and accepting my true self. I decided right from the start to accept and love myself for who I really am, without any doubts or reservations. It shows how committed I am to living a life without shame or criticism.

Throughout my whole life, I've been lucky to have the love and support of my dearest friends and family. Their presence has been a safe place for me that has given me the power and courage to be myself. In turn, this authenticity has not only changed my own life but has also inspired the people around me to find their own ways to express themselves and learn more about thcmselves.

In the big picture of my life, I've learned that life is an amazing journey of personal growth. It's like a beautiful tapestry where each thread represents the traits of patience, faith, and unwavering commitment. Every important thing that has happened to me in my life has helped me become the person I am today. Each part of my life's story has added to the depth and complexity that make me who I am. When I think back on the chapters of my life, I'm reminded of how strong the human spirit is and how important it is to take life's difficulties and successes in stride.

Key Lessons and Insights Gained

I am always surprised by the deep experiences that have changed me. From the lowest points of failure to the highest points of success, my story shows the tapestry of wisdom that has shaped my worldview, interactions, and general way of living. I became the person I am today by going through a lot of different things.

When I was young, I had a deep realisation that changed the course of my life. It became clear to me that empathy and care were very important guiding principles. I've gotten really good at making deep, important connections with the people around me over the course of my life. This amazing skill has grown and improved because I have never stopped trying to see the world from other people's points of view. During my journey, I've come to deeply understand that if I want to be a great friend, family member, and coworker, I need to build a strong foundation of understanding in myself. This is a very important quality that has helped me become an amazing person who can always support and understand those around me. Through the many seasons of my life, I've come to realise that this is something I understand.

From the moment I was born, it was clear that my life was going to be a collection of songs. Each chapter, verse, and refrain has been stitched together to make a large piece of music that is all mine. Throughout this incredible trip, one thing has stayed the same: the search for authenticity. As the story of my life started, I learned how important it was to be myself. I learned to harmonise with my inner voice, like a delicate tune, and let it lead me to a life where I could be myself. This discovery became the most important thing in my life, affecting every choice and action I made afterwards. With every step I took, I had to deal with the ups and downs of life's pace. The stuttering sounds of problems and problems No matter what pressures society puts on me from the outside, I have always stuck to the idea that I should stay true to my own personal values, beliefs, and hobbies. The life I've been given is a direct result of a key choice that allowed me to go against the flow of conformity and instead forge my own path based on unwavering honesty. This decision has given me a life that is full and has a sense of meaning.

Throughout my life, I've had to deal with a lot of tough situations that have helped me become who I am today. My journey will always be marked by these obstacles, which often came in the form of hard teachers. Every loss I had on my trip turned out to be a key step that helped me grow as a person and gave me more drive. These setbacks tried to show how strong I was and helped me get stronger, which pushed me towards the top of success. Over the course of my life, I've had failures and losses that have shaped me in a way that can't be erased. These events have taught me important lessons that have helped me become the person I am today. Like experienced teachers, they've taught me what I need to know to succeed in the future.

Over the course of my life, I've learned how important it is to live in the present and value the deep ties that mean a lot to me. I think about how life is like a complicated tapestry, with delicate threads of fleeting events and deep connections between people. From the depths of my soul, I've come up with a daily motto that speaks to the core of who I am. It serves as a constant reminder and pushes me to take advantage of all the wonderful experiences that life gives me. I work hard to live in the present moment, savouring every detail and learning from it. I also value the close relationships I have with my loved ones, knowing that they are priceless and taking care of them with all my love. When the world gives me chances, I take them with unwavering determination, determined to get every bit of potential out of them. This, dear reader, is the story of how I live my life every day.

When I think about the road I've taken so far, I feel a deep sense of gratitude for the amazing chances that have shaped and improved my life. Over the course of my life, I've been lucky enough to have a lot of different experiences that have helped me grow and change in important ways. Every event in my life, from the smallest baby steps to the biggest achievements, has helped me grow in more ways than I can count. Throughout my life, I've had to deal with a lot of problems that have helped me become the person I am today. These problems haven't stopped me from getting where I want to go; instead, they've helped me move forward on my path to personal growth and improvement. They have pushed me to get out of my comfort zone and become a stronger, wiser version of myself. All my life, I've been driven by a strong desire to be successful in both my personal and work life. This relentless quest has made me who I am and moved me forward, marking important points on my journey. Every win I've won shows how determined and determined-minded I am.

In my story, I think about how hard things are and how important they are in the big picture of life. These difficulties, like the spices in a dish, add flavour, depth, and personality to our lives. Throughout my life, I've been lucky to have the help and advice of amazing people who have had a big impact on who I am today. They have been my trusted guides and hardworking teachers.

They have given me advice and helped me along the path of personal growth and development. Their help has been very important to me, and I am grateful for how much they have changed my life. Throughout my life, I've faced many tests and obstacles that have helped me become the person I am today. These events have given me the strength and wisdom to face problems head-on and come out of them stronger and smarter. Each test I've had to go through has helped me grow as a person by pushing me to my limits and making me use my inner power. Not only have these tasks tested my physical and mental strength, but they have also made me think and understand myself more deeply. I have decided to see the hard things that have happened to me as chances to grow instead of giving in to them. Every mistake I've made has helped me learn more about myself and the world around me. Through these hard times, I've learned to change, keep going, and look for the good even in the worst situations. It wasn't easy for me to build up my strength. It has been shaped by a long history of fighting and difficulty. But as I've overcome problems, my determination has gotten stronger.

Throughout my life, I've had a lot of difficult times and had to deal with a lot of different problems. However, I've been lucky enough to have the unwavering support of a caring community. This community has been my compass, pointing me in the right way. When I was in trouble, the new knowledge I had gained helped me get through it. Over the course of my journey, I've come to understand how important my community is to me. It has been a steady base that has given me comfort and strength during the stormy times I've been through. The constant support and encouragement I've received from my community has been invaluable, giving me an unshakeable sense of comfort and security. I've learned this important lesson through the love of my family and the power of asking for help.

As I've moved through the working world, I've seen the ups and downs that make up the very core of life. When the author started their career, it was the beginning of a new part of their life that was full of new challenges and life-changing events. During this important time in my life, I set out on a trip to build a strong foundation in a place I didn't know. When I think about my trip, I remember the wise words of the well-known Les Brown. His classic saying, "You don't have to be great to start, but you do have to start to be great," spoke to me deeply at a turning point in my life. At the time, I was dealing with a lot of unknowns and responsibilities and didn't know how to handle the road ahead. But through the power of these words, I found a source of motivation that pushed me forward on a journey that changed my life. These words sparked a fire in me and made me even more determined to do what I needed to do. Even when doubt was on the horizon, they were a powerful reminder to be open to the unknown and start the journey to greatness.

As I worked my way up the complicated ladder of my job, I took every chance I could to improve my skills and grow as a person. I was at an intersection of trouble because I had to deal with a lot of problems. But my unwavering resolve led me forward and helped me overcome these problems, which made me stronger and more capable. As I went through life, I found that each new event helped me understand the world in a deeper and more meaningful way. Every new person I met and every new experience I had helped me grow as a person, expanding my skills and views.

When I think about how far I've come in my life so far, I feel a deep sense of thankfulness. The many different things that have happened to me and helped me become the person I am today, the problems I've solved, and the progress I've made make me feel so grateful. Resilience, tenacity, and unshakable courage are the threads that make up the tapestry of my life. I stand before you today as a live example of the unstoppable power of persistence. I've been through a lot of tough times and won a lot of victories. My journey has shown me how important it is to enjoy every precious moment of life with all my heart.

Personal Philosophy and Values

Over the course of my life, I've had a lot of different events that have shaped my own ideas and beliefs. These ideas help me decide what to do, how to act, and how to talk to other people. These rules come from my life up to this point, including how I was raised and what I've thought about when I've thought about what really matters.

My whole worldview is predicated on the premise that everyone should be treated with love, generosity, and respect. My entire life, I've attempted to comprehend what other people are going through. Whether we're talking or going through a difficult period, I try to see things from the other person's perspective. This method of thinking has enabled me to connect with others on a deeper level and cope with difficult situations in a compassionate and understanding manner.

Honesty and honesty have always been two of my highest priorities. Since I can remember, honesty and integrity have been essential to me. I believe it is critical to be honest and open in all of my interactions, and I strive to uphold these ideals in all aspects of my life. I've always tried to live my life by my ideals and beliefs.

I have always wanted to learn new things and get better since I was a child. This goal has been a constant in my life and has shaped both my personal and work goals. I have always thought that learning new things and growing as a person are very important. I'm sure that these are the things that will help you live a full and worthwhile life. By always trying to get better, I've been able to build a life that means a lot to me. My life has been driven by my desire to improve myself through deliberate self-improvement and the pursuit of new adventures.

I've always cared about my community and the work I do for free. As for me, I think it's important to make a good difference in the world. I try to teach the people around me what I know and how I know it. To do this, I have always tried to get active in local issues and give my voice and money to causes I care about.

Lord Krishna is a revered Hindu god whose lessons have had a big impact on my way of thinking. One of the most important things I've learned from my life is the value of emotional distance. This has changed the way I see relationships and exchanges with other people in a big way. In my narrative, I want to discuss what I know about true spiritual understanding. Krishna advised us not to be concerned with the consequences of our actions. This indicates that we should go about our work without expecting or wishing anything to happen. This allows us to achieve serenity and contentment inside ourselves, which is the ultimate purpose of spiritual life. I've seen how powerful this idea can be in my own life, and it's helped me get through challenges and problems with ease and grace. Through my experiences, I've learned useful things that have helped me deal with many problems.

As an avid reader of Krishna philosophy, I have always been drawn to Bhagavad Gita, a famous Hindu book that has won the hearts and minds of people all over the world. In its pages, the wise and respected Krishna taught me important lessons about not being attached. It really is one of the most important philosophical books ever written, and I'm glad I had the chance to study it. When I think about my life, I remember the important lesson that Krishna taught Arjuna in the Gita. My journey has been guided by the lesson that one should do their job without worrying about the results. I've come to understand how important it is to do things with a sense of duty and dedication, not just to make money or get noticed.

This understanding has greatly aided me in my career. As a rookie officer at SBI, I've had to overcome several obstacles and issues. There have been occasions in my life when I worked hard on a task but it did not match my own expectations. I've spent my entire life believing that my responsibilities are more essential than everything else. I've learnt not to be overly concerned about the consequences of my actions. Instead, I concentrate on executing my work as best as I possibly can. I was afraid of failing, but Krishna's lessons helped me get over that fear. I teach that mistakes are normal and that we shouldn't let them define us. Instead, I have always worked hard to do my jobs and trusted that God would take care of the rest.

I learned the value of kindness and empathy from what Krishna taught me. I've always thought that everyone should be treated with kindness and respect, no matter their background, religion, or income. Krishna's teachings, which have had a big effect on my life, made me even more sure of this. I try to live my life according to these values and to be kind and respectful to everyone I meet. In my book about myself, I would like to stress how important it is to be kind to all living things.

This lesson has changed my life outside of school in a big way. The lessons Krishna taught me have had a big impact on how I think about kindness and empathy. I've always cared about these things, but learning Krishna's teachings has given me a deeper understanding of how important they are. I have always tried to be kind and thoughtful throughout my life. I think it's important to treat everyone with care and to be polite at all times, no matter what. I have recently made a conscious effort to improve my actions in this area. I've been trying hard to be even more considerate of others and to treat everyone I meet with kindness and respect.

I've learnt to keep cool in the face of adversity thanks to what Krishna taught me. In my book, I discuss why I believe it is critical to maintain your cool under pressure. I always encourage my readers to keep a level head, whether things are going well or not. As I reflect on my life, I've realised that it's critical not to let either happiness or misery consume you. I've set a goal for myself to maintain my balance and sense of direction throughout my life. Instead of feeling overwhelmed or lashing out, I believe it is critical to approach each work with patience and acceptance.

This lesson has helped me a lot in my own life. There have been times in my life when I was faced with difficult situations or problems, and I had to fight the urge to give in to my feelings. Even though I've had a lot of problems, I've always tried to stay calm in high-stress situations by remembering what Krishna said about the value of equanimity.

Krishna's lessons on not being attached, having kindness, and being calm have had a big impact on how I see life. I have given myself the chance to get through hard times and move towards a more meaningful and satisfying life. I feel lucky to have had the chance to learn about these ideas, and I'm looking forward to learning more about them as I continue to grow.

I owe a lot to Lord Krishna's lessons in terms of what I think about life and how it works. I've been lucky to have had the teachings of nonattachment, compassion, and serenity guide me through my life and work. These ideas have helped me a lot in my personal and professional development. I'm glad that my experiences have given me information and insight, and I'm looking forward to getting to know them better over time.

Lastly, peace and taking care of myself are important parts of my life. I understand that putting my emotional, mental, and physical health first has been just as important as working hard and reaching my goals. I've always thought it was important to have a well-rounded life that lets me do well in both my personal and work goals. To do this, I've made a schedule that helps me stay focused and get things done while also giving me time for the things that are important to me.

In the end, my personal philosophy and values have been the compass that has guided me through life. They have guided my decisions and helped me make the most of my chances as they come up. I have held on to certain morals and beliefs throughout my life, which have helped me become the person I am today. I'm thankful for the things I've done that have helped me stay true to these ideas. From now on, I'm going to try to live my life by these beliefs and keep getting better as a person.

When I think about what I've done in my life and what I've accomplished, I'm filled with happiness and hope for what's to come. In the course of my life, I've been lucky enough to achieve a lot and go on a lot of trips that have taken me all over the world. But I'm well aware that my journey of self-improvement and achievement is far from over. When I think about what I've done in the past, I can't help but feel excited about all the chances I'll have in the years to come.

From the very core of my being, I've always had a strong desire to change and grow. One of my most significant and long-term goals in life has been to go on a journey of self-improvement and self-development. This good goal has become a guide star that shows me the way and shapes my future. From the beginning of my life, I have had a deep-seated belief in the limitless possibility of growth and development. This firm belief has led me everywhere I've gone and shaped the way my life has gone and the decisions I've made along the way.

Since I was a child, I've always been driven by a strong desire to find out about all the opportunities that lie ahead. This constant commitment has shaped my journey and helped me move forward in my search for self-discovery and personal growth. I look forward to the obstacles and chances that come my way every day, knowing that they are the key to reaching my full potential. My unwavering commitment to exploring drives me to push limits, break rules, and go into places that haven't been explored before. Through this ongoing quest, I have been on a constant quest for self-improvement my whole life, driven by an insatiable desire to learn and grow. I have attended various classes with great enthusiasm along my travels, wanting to learn new things and extend my horizons. I gladly participated in educational training, seizing any opportunity to develop my abilities and get new knowledge. I have also spent a lot of time diving into the depths of literature and thinking about the wisdom and insights I have learned along the way.

I have put forth a lot of effort during my career to accomplish a variety of objectives. My ambition has always been to become a renowned leader in my chosen area. My ambition has always been to use my influence for the greater good of society and to make a constructive impression on the world. Even when I was little, I wanted to make a difference in the world. I have made it my mission to use my unique set of skills and knowledge to make the lives of the people around me better. I have always had a strong belief in my skills, even from a young age. This unwavering belief has pushed me forward and helped me overcome many obstacles and go above and beyond many people's expectations. Today, as I stand on the edge of a new project, I am completely sure that I can reach this goal. Every step I take is fueled by the memories of past successes and the knowledge that I have the skills and drive to beat any challenge that comes my way. I am sure that I will finish projects in the coming years. This confidence comes from the fact that I am naturally creative, never give up, and work hard.

It's clear that both my professional and personal goals have always been of the greatest importance to me. From the moment I was born, I was always determined to be great. This determination drove me to aim for excellence in every part of my life, whether it was my work or the complex web of relationships I had with other people. Throughout my story, I have worked hard to improve myself and my career. I have devoted myself to getting better at what I do and learning more about the field I have chosen. My constant desire to be the best has been the driving force behind everything I've done. From the bottom of my heart, I've always had a strong desire to see all of the world's amazing places. I've always been excited by the idea of travelling around the world and experiencing the many different countries. It's as if every part of my soul wants to learn from the people who live in this beautiful world. In my never-ending chase of this lifelong dream, I have not only gone on many trips to far-flung parts of the world, but I have also taken steps to strengthen and value the relationships I have with other people. As I've tried to learn and understand more, I've come to realise how important it is to make real relationships with other people.

Curiosity and a drive to learn have been the threads that have connected my life. This persistent desire has driven me to abandon the security of my comfort zone and embrace the unusual and unfamiliar. I've had the opportunity to experience the kaleidoscope of human existence via my contacts with folks from various walks of life. Each person provides me with a unique perspective on the world, which helps me better comprehend it. When I think about the whole of my life, I'm humbled by the many things I've learned from the people I've met along the way. Their stories, traditions, and ways of life have become an important part of my own story and have changed who I am. I have always believed that travelling the world is the best way to learn and grow. I was drawn to the idea of learning about new cultures, trying food from other countries, and living in different places. I was so excited just to think about going on these trips that I couldn't find the words to describe it.

I'm reminded of the burning desire that has driven me since I was a child: an unquenchable thirst for adventure and a never-ending desire to learn about the many wonders of our world. This goal has been a steady light for me over the years, pointing me towards the amazing experiences that were waiting for me outside of my safe zone. Throughout my life, I have always put relationship-building with the people I care about most at the top of my list. I've always put a lot of value on these relationships because I think that having strong bonds with people you care about is important for a happy life. The times I've spent with my best friends and family in the comfort of my own home are moments I'll never forget. Since the beginning, I've always tried to build real, important relationships with the people I've met. I've known from a young age how important it is to take care of and value the ties that have helped me throughout my life. I have always put the importance of these connections first, whether it was by just spending quality time together, offering unwavering support during hard times, or just being present and paying attention.

It's clear that my hopes and goals have always been about the deep desire to find meaning and purpose in my very existence. From the bottom of my heart, I have always been sure that I am the only one who can change the way my life goes. This strong belief has kept me moving forward and given me the determination to overcome any obstacle that tries to stand in my way. With a strong commitment to excellence, a strong work ethic, and an unstoppable spirit, I've come to understand that when I set my mind to something, the possibilities are endless. As I think about my life, I feel more and more determined to follow my dreams. I, the author, start each day on a path of personal growth and improvement, ready to face the challenges that lie ahead. I am always excited about the many opportunities that the future holds, and I am working hard to make my dreams come true.

When I look back on my life and think about what I've learned, I think about what kind of mark I want to make on the world. Since the beginning of my life, I have always been aware of how much my actions affect the people around me. My whole life, I've been thinking about the same thing: what will people remember about me when I'm gone? When I think about the legacy I will leave behind, I wonder if I will be remembered as someone who made good changes in the lives of others or as someone who accidentally caused them pain. As I go on a trip of self-reflection, I uncover that the tapestry of my life has had a significant effect on the lives of everyone I've met.

Throughout my life, I've had the opportunity to witness how much my actions may impact the lives of others I care about. There have been moments when my decisions have brought them so much delight and happiness that their hearts have overflowed with joy. But I must acknowledge that there have been occasions when I made decisions that have harmed individuals I care passionately about. I've learned over the course of my life that everything I do can have a big effect on the world around me. This important understanding has taught me that it is my job to make sure that the results of my actions are always good. When people think about what I leave behind, I want them to remember me as someone who always tried to make morally sound choices. I want to be known as someone who always showed kindness, compassion, and a willingness to help.

Throughout my life, I've always wanted to be remembered as a person who changed the world and the lives of the people I met in a big way for the better. In the big picture of my life, I've come to realise that the best way to judge my character is not by what I say, but by what I do. I have always been very determined to improve myself and become the best form of myself. This unwavering dedication has pushed me to keep pushing my limits and aim for excellence in every part of my life. I knew from a young age that it was important to make a good difference in the world. I realised that my actions, no matter how small, could make changes happen. This made me more determined to help make the world a better place and leave a permanent mark. Every day makes me more determined to make the most of every chance that comes my way. I'm always looking for ways to learn, grow, and change as a person. I am committed to expanding my horizons and broadening my viewpoint, whether it's through personal growth, education, or having important experiences. I stay strong as I go through the ups and downs of life. When it comes time for me to depart this world, I want to be remembered as someone who made a lasting impact on the lives of individuals and the world as a whole. I've had a lot of anxieties since the beginning of my existence that haven't gone away. These concerns are built into the very fabric of who I am. These thoughts have been with me on every step of my life's journey, never leaving my side. They are like true friends. I've learned over the course of my life how important it is to spend a lot of time thinking about myself and giving careful thought to the things I'm thinking about. I am sure that this kind of thinking is necessary to fully understand and respect the importance of these ideas.

I've had several opportunities throughout my life to make a lasting influence on the lives of others. My ancestry includes the stories of the folks I've met along the road. Everyone I've encountered, from friends and family to coworkers and strangers, has been influenced in some manner by my presence. Through my interactions and relationships, I have been able to impact the lives of others around me. I have tried to help people in many ways, whether it was by hearing, giving advice and support, or just being an inspiration. When I need inspiration, I find comfort in thinking about the many ways I have left an indelible mark on the world, even if it was through small things. When I think back on my life, I can't help but feel incredibly grateful for all the knowledge and experiences that have made me who I am today.

There is one thing that stands out more than anything else: how much power I have to change the lives of those around me. It's a lesson I've learned through years of living and thinking about myself. I've learned that the power I have isn't always obvious or instant. Instead, it's a subtle force that can change people's lives in ways I never thought possible. As I start to think about myself, I am aware of how difficult my life is. I understand that the things I've worked on over time, like the seeds I've planted, haven't always paid off right away.

Throughout my life, I've been involved in a lot of projects, some of which lasted for years while others were never finished. Still, I, the author, have learned how important it is to be patient and never give up on my road to achieving my most important goals and dreams. From the bottom of my heart, I have always been sure that the effects of our actions, no matter how small they may seem, have the incredible power to change the way the world works. So, driven by an unwavering passion, I keep planting seeds, longing for the day when they will grow into beautiful works of art that are full of beauty and have deep meaning. I've learned over the course of my life that it's important to act with meaning and purpose, even when the results may not be clear right away.

Since the beginning of my life, I have been driven by a strong desire to stick to a set of core beliefs and ideals. Through the ups and downs of my life, I have found comfort and strength in these leading principles. They have always been there for me, giving me knowledge and clarity even when things were hard. With their unflinching support, I've been able to find my way through the dangerous waters of life and make decisions that have changed the course of my life. From the very beginning of my life, I have held on tightly to a set of values that have shaped me into the person I am today. I have lived my life by a set of beliefs that have helped me become the person I am today. Kindness, openness, honesty, and persistence have been the values that have guided my actions and choices. Not only have these beliefs affected how I interact with other people, but they have also been a big part of my own growth and development.

I've been fortunate to have had the guidance and support of outstanding individuals from an early age, who have helped me become who I am today. These incredible people have been by my side, providing me with guidance and support while I've faced several problems and taken advantage of numerous opportunities. Their constant presence and impact have helped me become the kind of person I'm proud to call myself. I have always stuck to a set of ideals that have helped me become who I am today. I knew from a young age that it was important to be kind to other people, even if I didn't know them. This trust in the power of kindness has helped me decide what to do and how to treat the people around me. Another thing that has made me who I am is my desire to try new things and see things from different points of view. I've always been willing to see things from different points of view and learn from them. This willingness to try new things has helped me see more of the world and learn more about it.

Honesty has always been one of the most important things to me, both in my relationship with myself and with other people. I truly believe that being honest is important, even when it's hard or uncomfortable. This commitment to being honest has made my personal and work relationships more trusting and real. I have always shown tenacity and resolve when things don't go my way. I've been trying through hard times, but I've always found the strength to keep going. This unwavering desire has helped me get through tough situations and reach my goals.

Kindness, openness, honesty, and a strong work ethic have always been guiding principles in my life. They have shaped who I am, assisted me in making decisions, and altered my behaviour in the world. I'm pleased these values have always been a part of my life since they have shaped who I am now. I'm grateful for the essential lessons I've learned and how much they've helped me become the person I am today. I've always tried to live by a set of ideals that are important to me. These ideas have governed my dealings with others, and I have always attempted to help those around me in a positive way.

Throughout my life, it's important to remember that I'm not perfect and that I have made my fair share of mistakes. Throughout my life, I've always seen failures as important chances to learn and grow. My story shows how personal growth can change a person and how that change can affect both the person and the world. My whole life, I've been driven by a strong desire to make myself and the world around me better. This natural longing has been a big part of making me who I am today.

As I think about how my life has gone so far, I come to the profound fact that I have always been full of hopes and dreams for the future. From the beginning, I've made every decision based on my strong desire to leave a good mark on the world. My biggest dream has always been to leave this world better than I found it. I have worked hard my whole life to leave a lasting memory that will outlast time. I knew from a young age that it was important to leave a mark on the world that would last long after I was gone. I set out on a journey full of desire and purpose because I was determined to do it. Every choice I made and action I took was based on one goal: to build something that would stand the test of time.

Since I was a youngster, I've had a great desire to inspire others to pursue their aspirations and leave a lasting impression on the world. My entire life has been driven by a deep desire to make a positive difference. Seeing people follow their passions with all of their hearts and achieve their goals with success warms my heart. From a very young age, I was sure that every person has the amazing ability to make a big difference in the world. This belief has been the driving force of my life. I have devoted myself to giving other people the tools they need to understand their own power to change. I've spent my whole life looking for ways to motivate and help the people around me. I have always tried to help people change for the better, whether it was through my words, deeds, or just by listening. Seeing the amazing changes that can happen when people are given the tools to reach their full potential has been nothing short of awe-inspiring. I have tried many different things in my quest to help other people. I have taken part in mentoring projects, where I had the chance to help and guide people as they found their own ways to make a difference. Aside from that, I have

During the course of my life, I have travelled through the vast landscape of human connections, slowly learning how powerfully these connections can affect the minds of the people involved. I've learned over the course of my life how important it is to make relationships with other people. These connections have an undeniable impact on who we become and how much control we have over the people in our lives.

Throughout my life, I've experienced profound realisations that have permanently altered my perspective. It's a big discovery that shows how much power and control the relationships we build with other people can have over our lives. I've learned over the course of my life that my relationships have a huge effect on who I am and the decisions I make.

Relationships with my family, friends, coworkers, and even strangers have helped me become the person I am today. My family was the most important part of my life when I was growing up. The love and support they gave me without conditions gave me a sense of connection and safety. Through the many happy and hard times, we all went through together, my family taught me the importance of being kind, strong and determined. Their constant presence in my life has given me strength and direction and helped me become the person I am today.

As I moved away from my family, I started to realise how important it is to connect with other people. Friends joined me on this trip called life, making me laugh, making me feel better, and giving me a shoulder to lean on. Each new friend I made taught me something new about the world and helped me see things from a different point of view. These friendships have taught me how important it is to be kind and reliable, and how beautiful it is to share experiences. At work, I've had the chance to work with a wide range of people. Every professional relationship I've had, from coworkers to mentors, has helped me grow and improve as a person. 's journey, I've come to the profound understanding that every relationship I've made has left a lasting mark on the world around me. Knowing how important human ties are, I've made a firm promise to keep building on the ones I already have. I'm also always looking for new ways to connect with people and make deep bonds with them.

From the time I was a baby, my parents taught me how to have a deep sense of empathy and a deep well of kindness. During my journey, I came to understand how important it is to leave a lasting mark on the world that goes far beyond my own life. It was a life-changing realisation that made me want to move beyond living for myself and find a cause bigger than my own.

As the years have gone by and I've gone through the stages of my life, I've slowly come to a deep realisation. 's journey, I realise something very important: kindness and generosity have been the most important factors in my way to happiness and success. As I've gone through life, I've come to understand that these values aren't just vague ideas, but rather powerful and useful tools that have helped me get through many of life's challenges.

I, [Your Name], have learned over the course of my life how important it is to care for others and take care of their needs. I've learned over the course of my life that showing compassion and helping the people around me has a big effect. This understanding has not only strengthened my relationships with other people but has also given me a deep sense of belonging. During my trip, I've come to a deep realisation that has become my life's guiding principle. I have been working hard to incorporate this understanding into every part of my life. I have always strongly believed that small acts of kindness can make a big difference in the world. Whether I was volunteering in my neighbourhood or just listening to a friend who was having a hard time, I have always tried to make a difference through these small things. I've realised that how well I understand the problems and achievements of individuals I care about has had a significant impact on my compassion growth. On my journey through life, I've learnt profound lessons that have altered my perspective on the world. One of the most essential lessons I've learnt is the value of kindness. In my personal life, I've learnt the value of modesty and how much we all rely on one another. I've realised throughout my life that everyone has the incredible capacity to influence the world for the better. This profound insight has had a significant impact on how I think and act. I've also realised that sharing is an important aspect of my personal growth and development. From the beginning of my youth, I was taught a very important lesson: the importance of being kind and not caring about myself. During those formative years, I learned how important it is to share, whether it was the treasured toys that decorated my room or the valuable moments of my short life. As time went on, I realised how important this lesson was, because it was during these times that I started to express myself by sharing my thoughts, ideas, and experiences with the people who were lucky enough to be in my company. I've learned over the course of my life how important it is to share. It has helped me make deep connections with other people, going beyond the surface and getting to the heart of important relationships that have lasted. I've learned the value of kindness and friendship over the course of my life. I learned early on how important it is to share and care for others. I have always believed in the power of giving, whether it was giving a stranger a meal or helping a friend who was in trouble. Growing up in a close-knit community, I saw, firsthand, how acts of kindness can change the way people feel and how a group feels as a whole.

My parents, who were big on kindness and compassion, taught me that we are all linked and that what we do can make a difference in other people's lives. As I became an adult, I took these lessons with me and looked for chances to help others whenever I could. Whether it was helping out at local charities or setting up fundraisers for causes I cared about, I have learned over the course of my life how important it is to teach certain values.

One of the most important things I've learned is that these values are really supported when people give freely of their time, skills, and money. Since I was young, I've always wanted to inspire and encourage others to make a lasting, good difference in the world. I have devoted my whole life to the noble goal of starting a powerful chain reaction of kindness and care. I work hard to plant the seeds of kindness, hoping with all my heart for a ripple effect that will reach every part of this huge world. As I think about my life's journey, I've come to one important realisation: giving to others is one of the most important lessons I've learned. During my journey, I've learned how important it is to be grateful for the good things that have happened to me. This profound understanding has given me a deep sense of gratitude and made me more aware of the moral obligation I have to help those who are less fortunate.

As I grew up in the connected society of today, I went on a trip of self-discovery that led me to discover: the importance of caring and sharing. In my story, I discuss how I came to realise that these ideals are more important than ever in today's world., I recognise that going through times of trouble and conflict often makes people feel alone and ignored, which is a common feeling., I recognise that one of the most important things that have shaped me into who I am is a strong belief in the power of acts of kindness and giving to build a sense of community and shared goals. My beliefs have changed a lot over the course of my life because of the many events and interactions I've had with other people.

Having seen it for myself, I now know how much even the smallest acts of kindness can change the world. I've seen firsthand how powerful these small actions can be because they start a chain reaction that affects people far beyond where they started. These acts of kindness have the amazing power to spread happiness and make people feel more connected to each other. I have made it a goal of my life to make a good difference in the world around me. Whether it's through my work with local charities, my constant support for causes that are important to me, or just lending a hand to someone in need, I've always tried to do my part to make society more caring and connected. By always sticking to this concept, I hope to make a better future for myself and the people around me.

I have set out on a deep journey of self-discovery and growth from the very core of my being. As the chapters of my life turned, I slowly realised how important it was to make deep relationships with the people around me. These connections, made with love and care, have become the most important thing in my life. In my efforts to make the world a better place, I have worked hard to leave a positive mark wherever I go.

Realising that even little actions can cause a ripple effect has fueled my determination to effect positive change. Every day, I am struck by how much power we have to influence our environment and better the lives of others. Nonetheless, despite the turmoil and uncertainty that are so frequently a part of life, I have found solace in the search for purpose.

I've been guided throughout my life by a set of beliefs that have had a significant influence on who I am now. These beliefs have served as a compass for me, guiding me through life's ups and downs and assisting me in finding my path. They have assisted me in developing my character and making life decisions. Since the beginning of my life, these beliefs have been a part of me, guiding my thoughts, actions, and relationships with other people. They have become a big part of who I am and how I see the world. As I look back on my life, I can see how these values have helped shape my beliefs and my personality. As I started out on the great adventure of life, I slowly learned how important it is to give a hand and plant seeds of kindness in the hearts of others. As I thought about my trip, it became very clear to me that if we all take action, we can make the world a better place for everyone.

As I think about how my life has turned out so far, I've come to understand that our true legacy is more than just a list of accomplishments and awards. Since the beginning of my life, I've been driven by a strong desire to leave a good mark on the world. My whole life, I've been thinking about how much of an effect I've had on other people's lives and how I've helped make the world a better place. People will remember me as someone who genuinely cared about the well-being of others. All through my life, I've always had a strong sense of duty and held myself responsible for what I did. I wanted to make a change and have a positive effect on the world around me, so I never gave up on this goal.

As I start my journey of self-reflection through the chapters of my life, I am overcome with a deep sense of gratitude for the many amazing people, fascinating places, and life-changing experiences that have shaped me into the person I am today. When I, the author of this story, take a moment to think about how my life has gone so far, I am amazed by the complex and colourful tapestry that has been made from many small moments.

Throughout my life, there have been times when the road ahead of me seemed impossible to overcome and the weight of the whole world seemed to be on my shoulders. In my story, these were the times when I had to dig deep and find the unshakable strength I needed to keep going and move forward on my life's journey. Throughout my life, I've had to deal with many problems that have tried my strength and determination. But I have never given up, even when things were really hard. I realise that my events have had a big impact on who I am today. I'm so thankful for the things they've taught me that I'll never forget. Along the way, I've faced a lot of obstacles that have tested my strength and determination. These hard times have helped me see and appreciate my own inner strength and drive. I am struck by the deep realisation that my mistakes and setbacks have had a huge impact on who I am today. Through my journey, I've learned that these things that some people might see as signs of weakness are amazing chances to grow as a person and teach me important lessons.

As I begin my path of self-reflection, I am filled with a strong sense of pride in the person I have become and the significant influence I have had on the lives of others around me. As I go on my journey of self-reflection, I'm struck by how much I've influenced the lives of others around me. I've been fortunate to have numerous opportunities to make a difference in my life. I'm grateful for all of these opportunities to make the world a better place. I find comfort in the fact that my choices have always been based on how deeply I believe and think about things. My story is a mirror of my core values and beliefs. It is based on the ideas of honesty, compassion, and empathy. Since the beginning of my life, I have been deeply committed to living by a set of core values that have led my every move. These ideas have become an important part of who I am. They shape how I go through life and affect the decisions I make every day.

When I think about my life, I feel hopeful about the future. When I think about all the possibilities ahead of me, I'm excited and looking forward to the trip that lies ahead. My goals and the big difference I want to make in the world have always been crystal clear to me from the start. I have always been sure that my life will leave a lasting mark on history. I am sure that my goal in this life is to leave a legacy that will inspire and motivate generations to come. I've been pushed from the start by a tremendous desire to make the most of the abilities bestowed upon me by a higher force. Even when I was young, I was resolved to use my innate abilities and skills for the greater good. Making the world a better place and leaving an everlasting impact on the lives of everyone I encountered became my life's ambition. I've always believed that if I worked hard, was motivated, and had a strong sense of purpose, I could achieve my objectives and leave a lasting impression on future generations.

During the time I've been alive, I've been on a fascinating journey that has been full of both challenges and wins. Throughout my life, I have grown a deep sense of gratitude for every event that has shaped me, every person who has left an indelible mark on my journey, and every valuable lesson I have had the chance to learn. From the moment I was born, I had a constant fire inside me that drove me forward with unwavering drive and a strong spirit. Even when I was young, I had a strong sense of purpose and a strong desire to leave a mark on the world that would never be erased.

My ambitions ran through my blood and drove everything I thought and did. I didn't want to be just average; I wanted to be great and live a life that was more than just average. This burning ambition to achieve led me to go past my boundaries, to reach for and seize the stars with unwavering devotion. But I wasn't only motivated by desire; I also believed in the strength of my convictions. I refused to modify my principles for the sake of convenience or social acceptance. My values were the compass that helped me make every choice, giving me a sense of direction. Throughout my journey, I have used these guiding principles as my constant compass points. They have always been there for me, guiding me through the twists and turns of life and leading me down the road I was meant to take. Every time I take a step, I'm reminded of how important these values are to my future. I've always been driven by a strong desire to make a difference in the world for the better. I knew from a young age how important education was and how it could give people power and change their lives.

With this in mind, I set out to gain an education, determined to learn new things and acquire skills that would allow me to contribute to society in a meaningful way. But I aspired to be more than a teacher. I recognised that genuine change frequently begins at the local level, in our own communities. I wanted to help those in need and give back, so I looked for methods to donate.

I worked hard to make a difference in the lives of others, whether it was by volunteering for local causes, organising community events, or just listening to individuals in need. But my drive to make a difference didn't end there. I felt a great feeling of obligation to speak up for issues that were in line with what I valued and believed. Whether I was working for social justice, the health of the environment, or equal rights, I made it my mission to raise awareness and act. I used my voice to make the opinions of the underrepresented heard and to challenge the status quo, trying to make the world a fairer and just place for everyone. I have never wavered in my commitment to live up to these standards in any part of my life. Every day brings something new. When I, the author of this story, think about the different parts of my life, I feel an overwhelming sense of hope and happiness. The things I've been through and the lessons I've learned have given me a strong belief in the bright future that lies ahead. My road through life has been full of amazing experiences that have helped me become the person I am today.